DINOSAUR RECORD BREAKERS

THIS IS A CARLTON BOOK

© Carlton Books Limited 2013

Executive Editor: Paul Virr
Senior Art Editor: Jake da'Costa
Design: Dynamo Limited
Cover Design: Jake da'Costa
Production: Claire Halligan

First published in 2011 by Carlton Books Limited
An imprint of the Carlton Publishing Group
20 Mortimer Street, London W1T 3JW

2 4 6 8 10 9 7 5 3 1

A catalogue record for this book is available
from the British Library.

ISBN: 978-1-78097-345-6
Printed in Dubai

DINOSAUR RECORD BREAKERS

AWESOME DINOSAUR FACTS
- **BIGGEST!**
- **FASTEST!**
- **DEADLIEST!**

DARREN NAISH

CARLTON KIDS

ABOUT THE AUTHOR

Dr Darren Naish is a palaeontologist and science writer specializing in dinosaurs and prehistoric creatures. When he's not busy digging up dinosaurs and ancient reptiles, he's writing about them! Darren is an Honorary Research Associate at the University of Portsmouth, UK.

New dinosaur discoveries are being made all the time, but there are still many things that we don't know about dinosaurs. Sometimes we can only make educated guesses about them, often by comparing dinosaurs with modern animals. For example, nobody is certain exactly how fast most dinosaurs could move, but experts can estimate their speed, based on how fast modern animals can run.

Dinosaur experts like Dr Naish sometimes need to use special words to describe dinosaurs, but you'll find these words explained in the glossary on page 128.

# CONTENTS

RECORD-BREAKING DINOSAURS

Between 230 and 65 million years ago (mya), some of the most amazing creatures ever to have lived ruled our planet. The most successful of these were a group of reptiles that lived on land - the dinosaurs!

Dinosaurs reached record-breaking sizes and many grew amazing body armour, horns, spikes and claws. In this book, we look at the strongest, fastest, biggest and deadliest dinosaurs - and some of the more unusual dinosaur records too.

🏆 DINOSAURS RULE!

Dinosaurs were the most successful animals on land for about 165 million years. No other single group of animals has been so important for so long. By comparison, humans have been around for just a few million years.

🏆 WHERE ARE THEY NOW?

The reign of the dinosaurs did not last for ever. Sixty five million years ago one of the biggest natural disasters of all time caused almost all of the dinosaurs to vanish. Dinosaurs didn't die out completely though: one group survived. We call them birds.

🏆 CHANGING PLANET

Dinosaurs appeared during the Triassic period about 230 mya, and they thrived and evolved during the following Jurassic and Cretaceous periods. Together, these three time periods are known as the Mesozoic Era (see below). The world underwent a huge number of changes during the Mesozoic Era and dinosaurs had to evolve to survive.

🏆 DINOSAUR TIMELINE

Dinosaurs and mammals evolve

Birds evolve

TRIASSIC PERIOD	JURASSIC PERIOD
250 mya	199 mya

145 mya

MESOZOIC ERA

🏆 DINOSAUR FAMILY TREE

One reason for the dinosaurs' record-breaking success was their ability to evolve (develop and change) very rapidly. Early in their history, dinosaurs split into two major groups: the beaked ornithischians ('or-nith-iss-key-ans') and the long-necked saurischians ('sore-iss-key-ans').

Both groups started out as small, two-legged animals with flexible necks, grabbing hands and slim legs. Over millions of years, dinosaurs became increasingly spectacular and record-breaking species evolved in both groups.

Ceratopsians   Pachycephalosaurs

Ornithopods

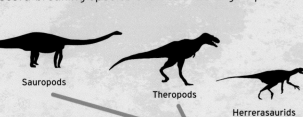

Stegosaurs   Ankylosaurs

Sauropods

Theropods

Herrerasaurids

Saurischians

Saurischians included the biggest dinosaurs of all (the long-necked sauropods) and the fearsome, meat-eating theropods.

Ornithischians

Ornithischians included record-breaking horned dinosaurs, spiky stegosaurs and the armour-plated ankylosaurs.

Dinosaurs

🏆 RIVAL REPTILES

Dinosaurs weren't the only prehistoric record breakers. Flying reptiles called pterosaurs and amazing marine reptiles shared the world with the dinosaurs and were also among the most amazing record breakers ever to evolve on Earth.

TRIASSIC

During the Triassic period the continents were united in a giant super-continent called Pangaea – the biggest landmass there has ever been. This allowed dinosaurs to spread far and wide across the planet.

Pangaea

CRETACEOUS

During the Jurassic and Cretaceous periods Pangaea broke up into smaller continents with different climates and plants. In turn, groups of dinosaurs split up and evolved into new species to suit their new surroundings.

North America   Asia
South America   Africa
Antarctica

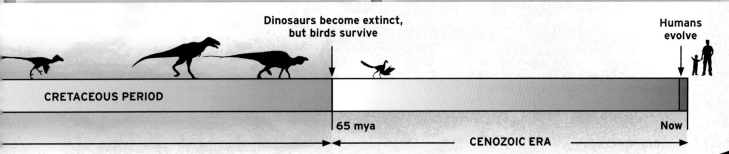

Dinosaurs become extinct, but birds survive

Humans evolve

CRETACEOUS PERIOD

65 mya   Now

CENOZOIC ERA

7

GOLDEN AGE OF DINOSAURS

Hundreds of different kinds of dinosaurs came and went during the 160 million years that they lived on Earth.

During that time span there were sometimes only a few different species living alongside each other. At other times there were many different kinds. Experts have worked out that a part of the Cretaceous period known as the Campanian age (between 83 and 70 mya) was the 'golden age of dinosaurs', boasting around 100 different types of dinosaur.

Several giant meat-eating dinosaurs lived in Campanian North America, including Albertosaurus (left), Gorgosaurus and Daspletosaurus. Perhaps they avoided competing with one another by hunting different prey.

During the Campanian age, high sea levels and flooding broke up the land into lots of smaller areas. The land animals split up across these different habitats and developed into new species.

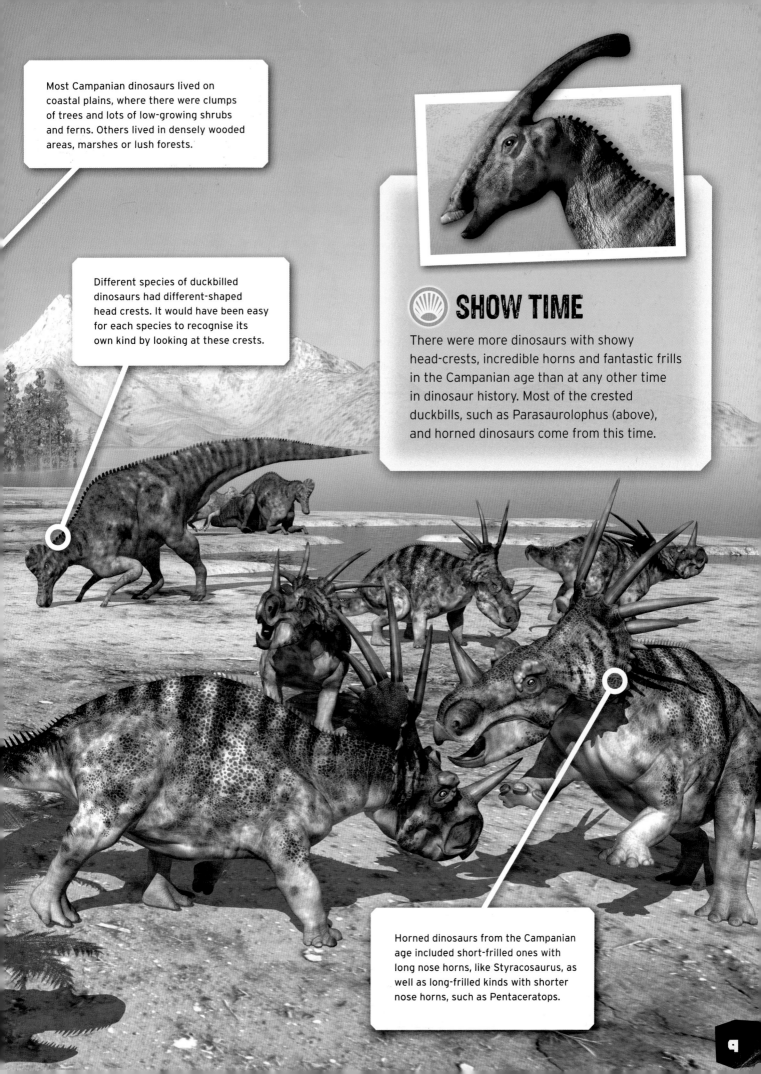

Most Campanian dinosaurs lived on coastal plains, where there were clumps of trees and lots of low-growing shrubs and ferns. Others lived in densely wooded areas, marshes or lush forests.

Different species of duckbilled dinosaurs had different-shaped head crests. It would have been easy for each species to recognise its own kind by looking at these crests.

SHOW TIME

There were more dinosaurs with showy head-crests, incredible horns and fantastic frills in the Campanian age than at any other time in dinosaur history. Most of the crested duckbills, such as Parasaurolophus (above), and horned dinosaurs come from this time.

Horned dinosaurs from the Campanian age included short-frilled ones with long nose horns, like Styracosaurus, as well as long-frilled kinds with shorter nose horns, such as Pentaceratops.

MOST FAMOUS

Most people easily recognise the body shape of Tyrannosaurus rex, with its big jaws and its two short arms.

TYRANNOSAURUS REX

Tyrannosaurus rex (tie-ran-oh-sore-us rex) is the most famous dinosaur ever, appearing in films, books and adverts worldwide.

One reason for its fame is the sheer size of this awesome predator. Another is its ferocious reputation as a killer. It simply sticks in people's minds. It was also one of the first giant meat-eating dinosaurs to be put on display in a museum.

FAME AND FORTUNE

Tyrannosaurus rex was first discovered in 1902 by palaeontologist (dinosaur expert) Barnum Brown (right). Since then, another 50 or so have been discovered, though many were incomplete. One of the best specimens - nicknamed 'Sue' - was found in South Dakota, USA, in 1990 and was sold at auction for $8.36 million!

Old pictures and museum mounted skeletons of Tyrannosaurus rex show it walking upright, dragging its tail. In fact, like most dinosaurs, it probably walked with its body and tail held horizontally.

MEET T.REX

Because Tyrannosaurus rex is so popular, it is the centrepiece of many museums worldwide. Some museums even have working robot models that roar and move.

TYRANNOSAURUS REX
(tie-ran-oh-sore-us rex)

WHEN	Cretaceous 67-65 mya
WHERE	USA, Canada
SIZE	12m long
WEIGHT	About 6 tonnes
DIET	Carnivorous
SPEED	up to 29km/h
DANGER	HIGH

For many years Tyrannosaurus rex held the record for the biggest meat-eating dinosaur, but it was knocked off the number one spot by Spinosaurus, discovered in 1912 (see p48/49).

⭐ SCREEN STAR

Tyrannosaurus rex has often played the role of villain in monster movies, from King Kong in 1933 to the Jurassic Park movies of more modern times. The Jurassic Park movies were so successful that they broke box-office records.

⭐ FAMOUS T.REX APPEARANCES

1933 ➡ **KING KONG**

1954 ➡ **GODZILLA**
MOVIE MONSTER BASED ON T. REX

1992 ➡ **BARNEY THE DINOSAUR**
TV SHOW, BASED ON T. REX

1993 ➡ **FIRST JURASSIC PARK MOVIE**
T. REX EATS PEOPLE ON SCREEN

1997 ➡ **JURASSIC PARK**
THE LOST WORLD MOVIE

SUPER HEAVYWEIGHT CHAMPION

AMPHICOELIAS

Plant-eating dinosaurs known as sauropods had extremely long tails and necks and were often enormous, but one giant called Amphicoelias (am-fee-see-lee-us) out-sized all the others.

Only two of this plant-eater's bones have been found so far, but scientists have used them to work out that it was the biggest land animal that ever lived.

Amphicoelias was so big that it would have had to feed on hundreds of kilograms of plant food every day. It must have lived in places where there were lots of shrubs and trees.

The sheer size of Amphicoelias would have protected it from most predators.

AMPHICOELIAS
(am-fee-see-lee-us)

WHEN	Jurassic 155-145 mya
WHERE	USA
SIZE	40-60m long
WEIGHT	About 70-100 tonnes
DIET	Herbivorous
SPEED	16km/h
DANGER	MEDIUM

BIGGER THAN A WHALE

Amphicoelias was longer than a blue whale, but not as heavy. With its long neck, this dinosaur was tall enough to reach the treetops to feed. Amphicoelias could even have stood on its hind legs to reach higher, using its tail as a prop. Then again, it was also strong enough to simply push the trees over. It would have certainly made the ground shake when it walked!

To get this big, Amphicoelias would have to spend a lot of its time eating, stripping the leaves off trees with its pencil-shaped teeth.

HOW HEAVY?

Awesome Amphicoelias weighed up to 100 tonnes - that's as much as 20 African elephants.

=

10

5

0

metres

SUPERSIZE SAUROPOD

One of the Amphicoelias bones discovered is from the spine and is over 2 metres tall! Part of a thigh bone was also found. This piece of bone suggests that Amphicoelias had back legs that were up to 9 metres long - that's as tall as two giraffes.

FASTEST RUNNER

STRUTHIOMIMUS

The fastest dinosaur runners were the long-tailed ostrich-like dinosaurs such as Struthiomimus (strooth-ee-oh-mime-us).

It's possible that this high-speed dinosaur could run at speeds of up to 80 kilometres per hour. That's nearly as fast as a racehorse! Struthiomimus had to be speedy to escape from fast-moving predators such as Gorgosaurus.

A long tail helped Struthiomimus to balance and to make quick turns while running.

BUILT FOR SPEED

Struthiomimus had long slender legs, but with powerful thigh muscles to help it run fast. In modern-day ostriches, hip and leg muscles make up about a third of the animal's weight. This figure might have been even higher in ostrich dinosaurs. The same muscles make up about one-fifth of a human's weight.

LAND SPEED RECORD

Here's how modern-day fast-running land animals compare with Struthiomimus.

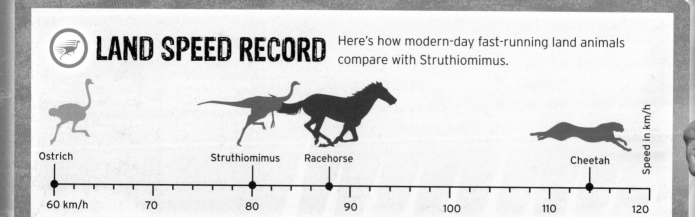

Ostrich   Struthiomimus   Racehorse   Cheetah   Speed in km/h

60 km/h   70   80   90   100   110   120

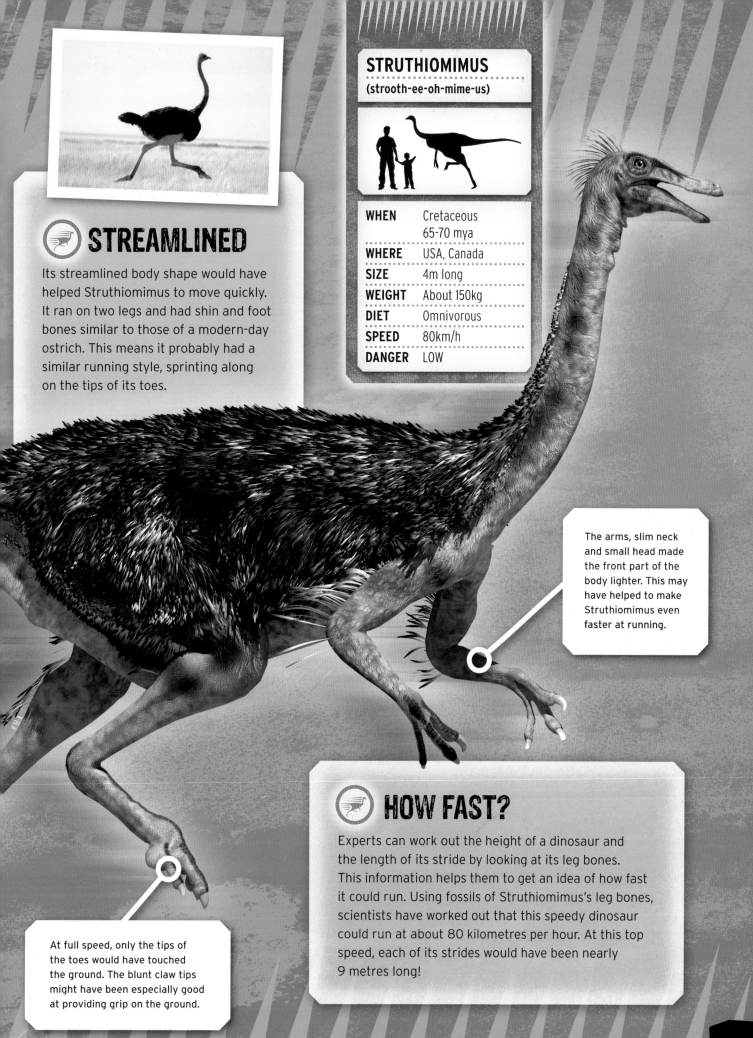

STREAMLINED

Its streamlined body shape would have helped Struthiomimus to move quickly. It ran on two legs and had shin and foot bones similar to those of a modern-day ostrich. This means it probably had a similar running style, sprinting along on the tips of its toes.

STRUTHIOMIMUS
(strooth-ee-oh-mime-us)

WHEN	Cretaceous 65-70 mya
WHERE	USA, Canada
SIZE	4m long
WEIGHT	About 150kg
DIET	Omnivorous
SPEED	80km/h
DANGER	LOW

The arms, slim neck and small head made the front part of the body lighter. This may have helped to make Struthiomimus even faster at running.

HOW FAST?

Experts can work out the height of a dinosaur and the length of its stride by looking at its leg bones. This information helps them to get an idea of how fast it could run. Using fossils of Struthiomimus's leg bones, scientists have worked out that this speedy dinosaur could run at about 80 kilometres per hour. At this top speed, each of its strides would have been nearly 9 metres long!

At full speed, only the tips of the toes would have touched the ground. The blunt claw tips might have been especially good at providing grip on the ground.

BIGGEST HEAD

PENTACERATOPS

The North American horned dinosaur Pentaceratops (pen-ta-serra-tops) probably had the biggest head of any land animal that ever lived.

Including its enormous frill, this plant-eater's awesome head was as long as a small car.

 BIG HEAD

Why did Pentaceratops have such a big head? One theory is that, like a satellite dish, the size and shape of the frill helped to collect sound and so gave the dinosaur better hearing. Good hearing would have helped Pentaceratops to keep alert to predators.

Each species had its own unique shape of frill, which may have helped them to recognise each other.

PENTACERATOPS
(pen-ta-serra-tops)

WHEN	Cretaceous 71-75 mya
WHERE	USA
SIZE	7m long
WEIGHT	About 5 tonnes
DIET	Herbivorous
SPEED	32km/h
DANGER	LOW

 COOLING OFF

Modern elephants flap their enormous ears to cool their blood as it passes through. In the same way, some horned dinosaurs may have used their huge frills to get rid of heat and to control their body temperature – just like a radiator gives off heat!

Finger-shaped bony lumps were arranged around the edges of the frill. These seem to have been decorative and were different from one horned dinosaur to the next.

The frill was not separate from the skull. It was made of skull bones that stretched backwards and outwards.

SHOW OFF

The huge frill of Pentaceratops was not a thick, solid shield of bone. In places it had large oval-shaped openings or holes, covered with skin. For this reason, it would not have been tough enough to use as a shield to fend off predators. It is more likely that the frill was used for showing off. It may even have been decorated with stripes or spots.

MOST MISUNDERSTOOD DINOSAUR!

CITIPATI

When new discoveries are made, experts sometimes have to change their minds about dinosaurs. As a result, some dinosaurs have very mixed-up histories – and the most muddled of all is Citipati (sit-ee-pat-ee).

When it was first discovered, Citipati was mistaken for its close relative, Oviraptor, because they looked so similar. Citipati's discovery also revealed that a nest of eggs, once thought to belong to Protoceratops actually belonged to Oviraptor. Confused? You should be!

EGG THIEF?

Some modern-day animals, such as crows, steal eggs to eat. So when an Oviraptor was discovered with eggs thought to belong to Protoceratops, experts thought Oviraptor was an egg thief too. That's where its name, meaning 'egg thief' comes from. Later, it turned out that the eggs really belonged to the Oviraptor, so it wasn't an egg thief after all. Then a new Oviraptor specimen, nicknamed 'Big Mamma', was discovered sitting on a nest of eggs, just like a modern bird. It eventually turned out that 'Big Mamma' was actually a new type of dinosaur. Scientists named it Citipati.

We can tell from fossils of similar dinosaurs that Citipati probably had large feathers on the hands and a large feathery tail fan.

Citipati had a hollow, bony head crest, which was probably covered in a tough horn-like material.

CITIPATI
(sit-ee-pat-ee)

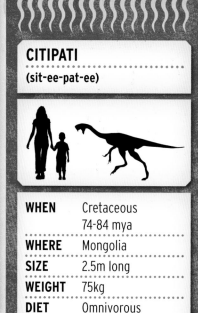

WHEN	Cretaceous 74-84 mya
WHERE	Mongolia
SIZE	2.5m long
WEIGHT	75kg
DIET	Omnivorous
SPEED	48km/h
DANGER	NONE

WHAT'S FOR DINNER?

Citipati had a short, deep head with bony prongs on its palate (the roof of its mouth). Some experts think this head design was suited to eating shellfish, or that like ducks these dinosaurs swam and caught food in lakes. Others have suggested that Citipati ate leaves, or hunted small animals. It's possible they did all these things.

EGGS AND BABIES

Citipati arranged its eggs in a circle. The mother probably laid two eggs a day over many days. Fossil babies found inside unhatched eggs have well-developed leg bones, so they were probably able to run around within minutes of hatching, like the chicks of modern-day pheasants.

SORTING OUT CITIPATI

Here is a timeline showing the confusing history of this dinosaur...

| 1920 | 1930 | 1940 | 1950 | 1960 | 1970 | 1980 | 1990 | 2000 |

1 Oviraptor is discovered with 'Protoceratops' eggs and thought to be an egg thief.

2 A 'Protoceratops' egg is discovered containing an Oviraptor baby, so it turns out Oviraptor is not an egg thief after all.

3 A large 'Oviraptor' called 'Big Mamma' is found on top of a nest of eggs.

4 It is realised that 'Big Mamma' and the eggs are not Oviraptor, but a new dinosaur - Citipati.

MOST BABIES

PSITTACOSAURUS

A truly amazing fossil of the beaked dinosaur Psittacosaurus (sitt-ack-uh-saw-rus) was discovered lying next to a record-breaking group of 34 babies.

Some dinosaurs may have produced even bigger families, but finding an adult together with its babies is very rare. No other dinosaur has ever been discovered with so many babies.

The fossilised adult was found lying right next to the babies and some of the babies might have been lying on top of it. This suggests a close relationship between the parent and its young.

 ## GOOD PARENTS?

The fact that there were so many babies found together suggests that baby psittacosaurs gathered in large groups and that the parents looked after them while they were small. Like some modern crocodiles and lizards, one or both parents may have guarded the babies, protecting them from predators and leading them to feeding areas.

Like most baby animals, young psittacosaurs had big, rounded heads.

PSITTACOSAURUS
(sitt-ack-uh-saw-rus)

WHEN	Cretaceous 105-115 mya
WHERE	Mongolia
SIZE	1m long
WEIGHT	About 6kg
DIET	Herbivorous
SPEED	Up to 40km/h
DANGER	LOW

SHARING CARING

It is possible that the 34 babies belonged to more than one adult Psittacosaurus. Some modern animals like penguins practise a behaviour called crèching, where one or two parents look after the young of many families. Maybe Psittacosaurus did this too.

SUDDEN DEATH

Because all 34 babies and the one adult were found close together, with their skeletons in good condition, they must have died quickly. Maybe they were buried by the collapsing roof of a burrow, or covered and suffocated by volcanic ash.

Some small, plant-eating dinosaurs dug burrows and kept their babies safe inside a large nest chamber. Maybe Psittacosaurus did this too.

FIRST FOSSIL PREDATOR

MEGALOSAURUS

Megalosaurus (meg-al-oh-saw-rus) was the very first dinosaur recognised by science. It was discovered in England over 300 years ago in the late 1700s.

Today we know that big predatory dinosaurs like Megalosaurus were two-legged animals with clawed, grabbing hands, but the scientists who first studied the bones were very puzzled by what they had found.

When Megalosaurus was first discovered, experts thought that its long, heavy tail dragged along the ground like that of a giant lizard. Later discoveries showed that the tails of just about all dinosaurs were actually held up in the air.

NUMBER ONE

A palaeontologist called William Buckland was the first person to study the remains of Megalosaurus and even gave the dinosaur its name. The remains were a mixture of bones belonging to several megalosaurs of different ages and sizes, including part of a lower jaw, with several of its curved, serrated teeth still in place. Buckland could see this new beast was a fierce predator, even if he didn't know exactly what it was.

THE FIRST DISCOVERIES

1824 → MEGALOSAURUS
1825 → IGUANODON
1833 → HYLAEOSAURUS
1836 → THECODONTOSAURUS
1837 → PLATEOSAURUS

MEGALOSAURUS
(meg-al-oh-saw-rus)

WHEN	Jurassic 164-167 mya
WHERE	England
SIZE	6m long
WEIGHT	700kg
DIET	Carnivorous
SPEED	48km/h
DANGER	HIGH

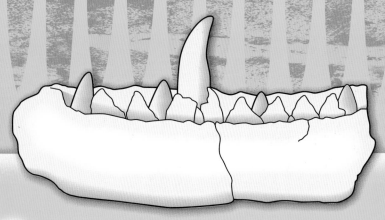

🦖 MEGA LIZARD

The lower jaw that was first found looked similar to the jaw bones of modern monitor lizards, so it was thought that Megalosaurus was shaped like a huge lizard walking on all fours. During the 1850s the 'giant lizard' idea gave way to the idea of a reptilian elephant, with four column-like legs and a short body and tail. Both were wrong.

Megalosaurus had powerful arms and may have used them to help keep prey animals still while it bit them.

🦖 BIG BITER

Fossils of other predatory dinosaurs, mostly from North America, eventually showed that Megalosaurus and its relatives were not lizard-shaped, nor did they walk on all fours. Instead they were two-legged predators with short arms and three large hand claws. They probably killed plant-eating dinosaurs by grabbing them with their clawed hands and taking slashing bites with their serrated teeth.

SMALLEST PREDATOR

ANCHIORNIS

At just 40 centimetres long, feathered Anchiornis (an-kee-orr-nis) from China holds the record for being the smallest known predatory dinosaur.

It would have weighed about 250 grams and was the size of a pigeon. A few other predatory dinosaurs - like Epidendrosaurus and Epidexipteryx - may have been smaller, but no fully grown adults have yet been found, so they can't qualify for the record.

🔍 MINI HUNTER

At first it was thought that Anchiornis was a type of ancient bird, but it's actually a bird-like dinosaur and a close relative of Troodon (see p30/31). Like most bird-like dinosaurs, it had long grasping hands and sharp, closely packed teeth. It was probably a speedy hunter of lizards and insects.

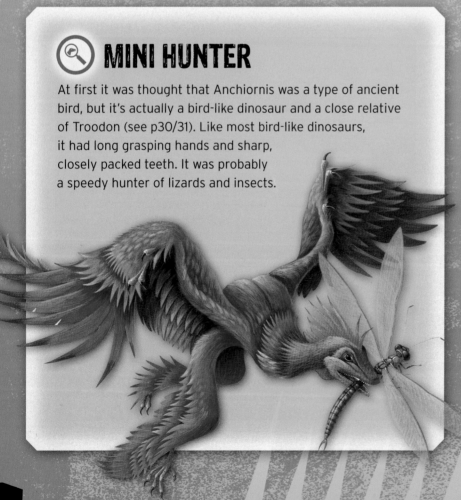

ANCHIORNIS
(an-kee-orr-nis)

WHEN	Jurassic 165-155 mya
WHERE	China
SIZE	40cm long
WEIGHT	250g
DIET	Carnivorous
SPEED	Up to 40km/h
DANGER	NONE

TOP 5 TINIEST DINOSAURS

1 → **ANCHIORNIS** → ABOUT 40cm LONG
2 → **PARVICURSOR** → ABOUT 45cm LONG
3 → **CAENAGNATHASIA** → ABOUT 45cm LONG
4 → **MEI LONG** → ABOUT 45cm LONG
5 → **MAHAKALA** → ABOUT 50cm LONG

DINKY DRAGON

In recent years, scientists have found quite a few new tiny predators, mostly in China and Mongolia. One of these is named Mei long. It was only about 45 centimetres long and the only known specimen was preserved curled up, as if asleep. This explains its name - it means 'soundly sleeping dragon'.

Thanks to its small size and long feathers, Anchiornis could probably glide or flap its wings. It might have jumped around on tree branches.

Sharp teeth and a slender snout suggest that Anchiornis preyed on small lizards and large insects.

The three long, slender, clawed fingers were mostly hidden by long arm and hand feathers.

MOST FEARSOME SEA PREDATOR!

LIOPLEURODON

Liopleurodon (lye-oh-pluur-oh-don) – a short-necked plesiosaur the size of a male sperm whale – wins the title of the ultimate ocean-going predator.

Bite marks preserved on fossil bones show that this sea monster attacked and ate other huge sea reptiles, sometimes biting them into pieces. Some experts calculate that its bite was perhaps ten times stronger than that of Tyrannosaurus rex!

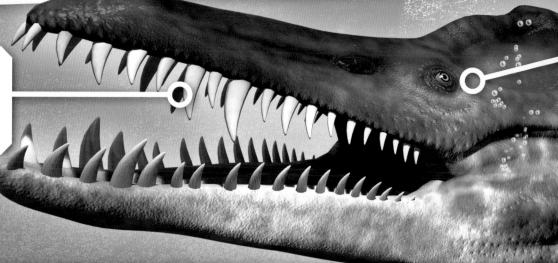

The pointed, gently curved teeth were deep-rooted in the jaws. They were perfect for grabbing struggling prey and for cutting into flesh.

POWER BITE

Liopleurodon probably took prey by surprise, rushing it at speed and attacking with an open mouth. It could have bitten off the paddles of other plesiosaurs, wrenching them clean off the body. Huge muscles at the back of its head powered its long, crocodile-like jaws. Its banana-shaped teeth were up to 30cm long.

🏊 GIANT KILLERS

Remains of Liopleurodon show that it definitely reached 6 metres in length, but small bits of fossilised bone from the lower jaw and back suggest that it could have been up to 15 metres long! By comparison, a modern-day killer whale is almost 10 metres long and the largest great white shark was 7 metres long.

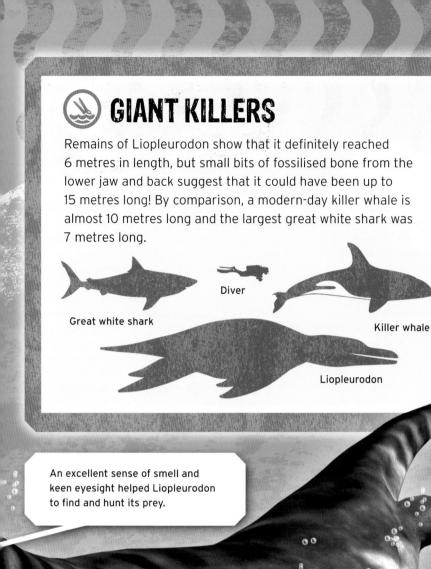

Diver

Great white shark

Killer whale

Liopleurodon

WHEN	Jurassic 165-145 mya
WHERE	England, France, Germany
SIZE	15m long
WEIGHT	6 tonnes
DIET	Fish, squid, marine reptiles
SPEED	Up to 7km/h
DANGER	HIGH

An excellent sense of smell and keen eyesight helped Liopleurodon to find and hunt its prey.

Fossilised stomach contents show that giant plesiosaurs such as Liopleurodon ate fish, swimming molluscs, other plesiosaurs, and the floating dead bodies of land animals like dinosaurs.

🏊 DEADLY AMBUSH

Because of its huge size, Liopleurodon would have taken care not to get stranded in shallow water. However, it may sometimes have taken a risk to catch prey. It is a very real possibility that it grabbed paddling dinosaurs and pulled them into deep water. Today, Killer whales hunt in this way. They rush up beaches and snatch sea lion pups from the water's edge.

MOST VALUABLE!

ARCHAEOPTERYX

The first bird ever found, Archaeopteryx (ar-kee-op-terr-ix), is one of the most valuable fossils of all time.

It is also one of the most important, since it was a crucial piece of evidence showing that birds evolved from small, predatory dinosaurs. Ten fossils have been found so far, and are regarded as the most valuable of all dinosaur finds. Specimens are worth around £10 million each.

 ## BEAUTIFULLY PRESERVED

Archaeopteryx lived near lagoons where the soft mud was perfect for preserving fossils. All of the Archaeopteryx specimens found so far were discovered in a layer of rock from one of these lagoons. This rock, called the Solnhofen limestone, is made up of tiny, smooth mud particles that once settled on the lagoon floor. The bodies of animals that fell in were beautifully preserved by the mud, revealing lots of fine detail, including feathers and teeth.

ARCHAEOPTERYX
(ar-kee-op-terr-ix)

WHEN	Jurassic 150-155 mya
WHERE	Germany
SIZE	50cm long
WEIGHT	500g
DIET	Carnivorous
SPEED	48km/h
DANGER	NONE

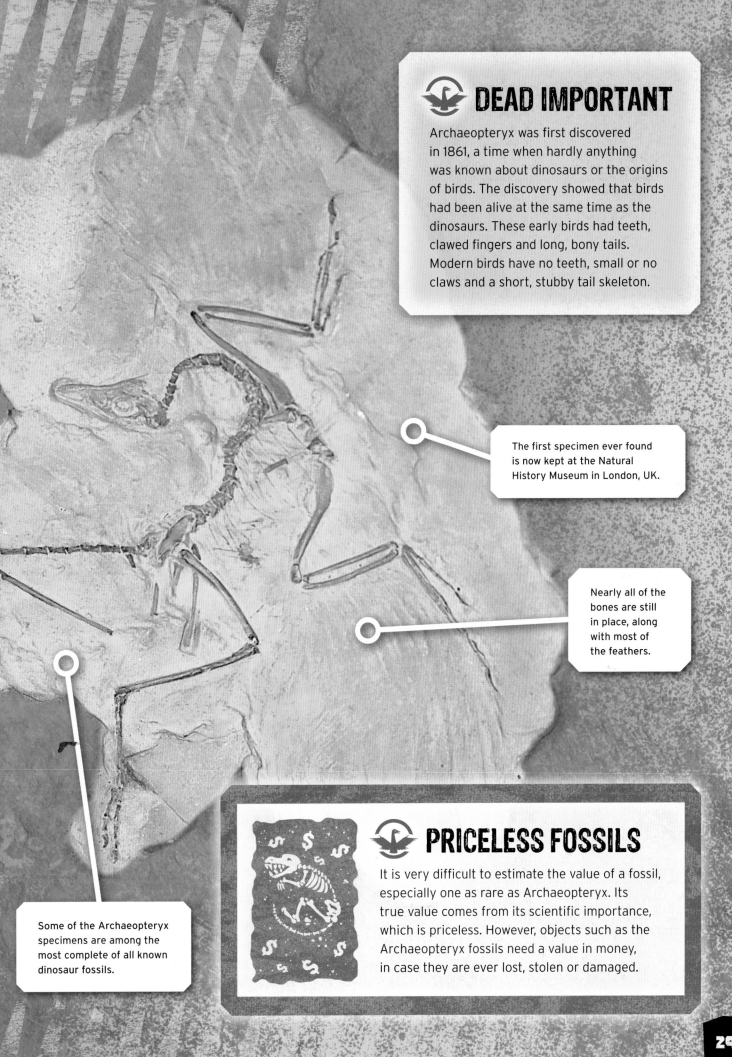

DEAD IMPORTANT

Archaeopteryx was first discovered in 1861, a time when hardly anything was known about dinosaurs or the origins of birds. The discovery showed that birds had been alive at the same time as the dinosaurs. These early birds had teeth, clawed fingers and long, bony tails. Modern birds have no teeth, small or no claws and a short, stubby tail skeleton.

The first specimen ever found is now kept at the Natural History Museum in London, UK.

Nearly all of the bones are still in place, along with most of the feathers.

PRICELESS FOSSILS

It is very difficult to estimate the value of a fossil, especially one as rare as Archaeopteryx. Its true value comes from its scientific importance, which is priceless. However, objects such as the Archaeopteryx fossils need a value in money, in case they are ever lost, stolen or damaged.

Some of the Archaeopteryx specimens are among the most complete of all known dinosaur fossils.

BIGGEST EYES

TROODON

The dinosaur that holds the record for the biggest eyes is the bird-like predator, Troodon (troo-uh-don), found in North America.

Each of its eyeballs was up to 4.5 centimetres wide – similar in size to those of an ostrich. Its giant eyes probably helped it to hunt at night.

Modern-day hunters such as cats have pupils that can change shape. In bright light they narrow to slits, to keep glare out. In darkness they become round, to let light in. Troodon's eyes probably did this too.

NIGHT SIGHT

Animals that hunt at night, such as owls, often have enormous eyes, but many animals active in the day also have large eyes – so eye size doesn't really tell us when an animal is awake and hunting. However, we know that some Troodon lived in the far north of the world, inside the Arctic Circle. This area is dark all day and night for months during the winter, so Troodon would have had to be able to hunt in the dark to survive.

The snout was narrower than the back of the head where the eyes were. This helped Troodon to see in front as well as to the sides.

Like birds and crocodiles, Troodon would have had upper and lower eyelids, and an extra third protective eyelid called the nictitating membrane.

 ## SUPER SPOTTER

The shape of Troodon's eye sockets tells us that it had binocular vision. This means that the fields of vision of both eyes overlapped in front of the animal's snout. Humans have binocular vision, and so do predators such as owls and cats. It enables animals to be especially good at judging distance - a very useful skill when hunting prey.

WHEN	Cretaceous 70-65 mya
WHERE	USA, Canada
SIZE	2.5m long
WEIGHT	35kg
DIET	Omnivorous
SPEED	Up to 48km/h
DANGER	MEDIUM

 ## SCARY STARE

Fossil dinosaur eyeballs are hardly ever preserved, so we don't really know what Troodon's eyes looked like. The colour of the iris (the coloured part of the eye) would have made a big difference to the way it looked. Owls that hunt during the day tend to have yellow irises, while those that hunt at night usually have dark irises. Perhaps this rule applied to Troodon, too.

GIANT EYE CHART

Compare the size of Troodon's eyes with some modern animals.

1 ➡ **GIANT SQUID** ➡ 25cm WIDE
2 ➡ **BLUE WHALE** ➡ 15cm WIDE
3 ➡ **OSTRICH** ➡ 5cm WIDE
4 ➡ **TROODON** ➡ 4.5cm WIDE
5 ➡ **HUMAN** ➡ 2.5cm WIDE

Human   Troodon   Ostrich   Blue whale   Giant squid

FIRST FOSSIL PLANT-EATER

IGUANODON

Iguanodon (ig-wan-oh-don), named in 1825, was the very first plant-eating dinosaur recognised by science.

To the early scientists who discovered them, dinosaurs were surprising, strange and difficult to understand. This was especially true because the earliest fossils - like those of Iguanodon - were just bits and pieces. Iguanodon was first known from just its teeth, which were similar to those of modern iguana lizards, but much bigger.

FINDING THE FOSSILS

We know that Gideon Mantell - a medical doctor and fossil expert - was the first person to get hold of the Iguanodon teeth and bones. It's often said that his wife Mary actually discovered the fossils. Others say that local quarrymen found them and then sold them on to Mantell.

For a while, Iguanodon was pictured as a kangaroo-like dinosaur that walked on two legs. Today we think that it often walked on all fours.

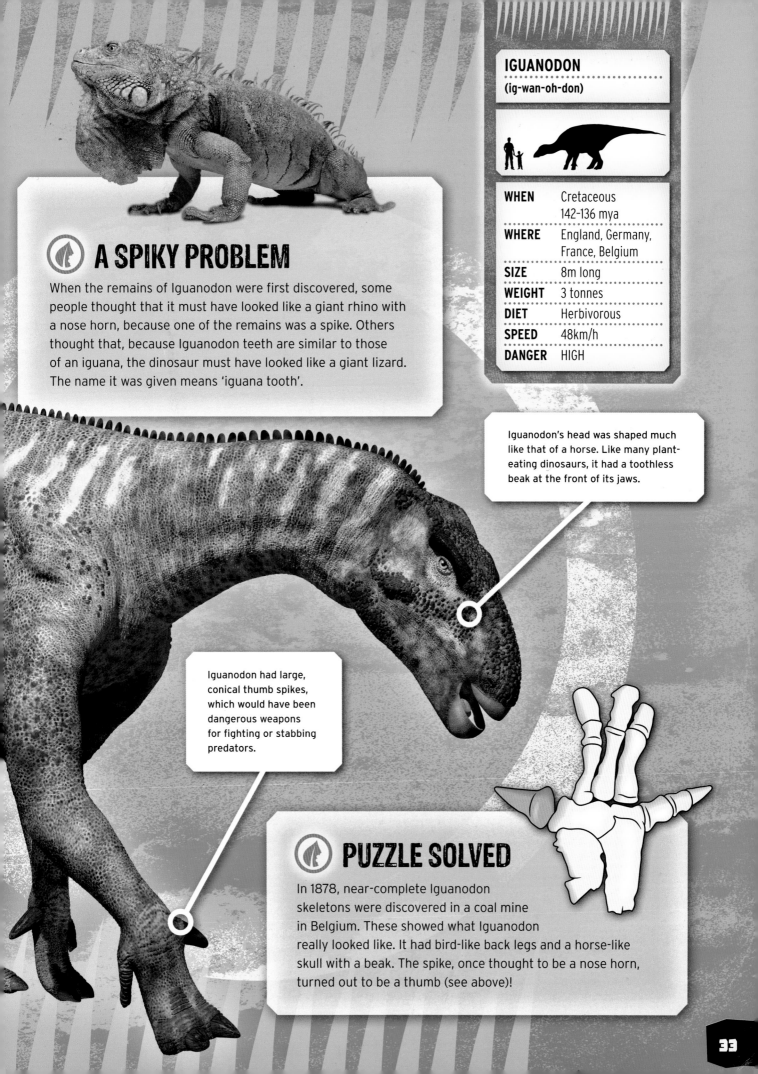

IGUANODON
(ig-wan-oh-don)

WHEN	Cretaceous 142-136 mya
WHERE	England, Germany, France, Belgium
SIZE	8m long
WEIGHT	3 tonnes
DIET	Herbivorous
SPEED	48km/h
DANGER	HIGH

A SPIKY PROBLEM

When the remains of Iguanodon were first discovered, some people thought that it must have looked like a giant rhino with a nose horn, because one of the remains was a spike. Others thought that, because Iguanodon teeth are similar to those of an iguana, the dinosaur must have looked like a giant lizard. The name it was given means 'iguana tooth'.

Iguanodon's head was shaped much like that of a horse. Like many plant-eating dinosaurs, it had a toothless beak at the front of its jaws.

Iguanodon had large, conical thumb spikes, which would have been dangerous weapons for fighting or stabbing predators.

PUZZLE SOLVED

In 1878, near-complete Iguanodon skeletons were discovered in a coal mine in Belgium. These showed what Iguanodon really looked like. It had bird-like back legs and a horse-like skull with a beak. The spike, once thought to be a nose horn, turned out to be a thumb (see above)!

BIGGEST CLAWS!

Therizinosaurus had a toothless beak at the front of its jaws and small, leaf-shaped teeth farther back for munching on plants.

THERIZINOSAURUS

Therizinosaurus (thair-ee-zine-uh-saw-rus) is one of the weirdest-looking dinosaurs ever found.

It was a giant two-legged, feathered plant-eater with a long neck and a big round belly. But its most incredible feature was its record-breaking claws, which may have been up to a metre long. There were three on each hand.

 ## SUPER SLASHERS

When it was alive, Therizinosaurus would have had a horny covering over the top of its claw bones. Its longest bone claw measured about 70 centimetres, but the horny covering would have made the actual living claw much longer. The claws were long, slender and gently curved, like a sabre sword.

THERIZINOSAURUS
(thair-ee-zine-uh-saw-rus)

WHEN	Cretaceous 70-65 mya
WHERE	Mongolia
SIZE	10m long
WEIGHT	About 5 tonnes
DIET	Omnivorous
SPEED	32km/h
DANGER	MEDIUM

 ## TOP 5 CLAW CHAMPIONS

Here are the top five dinosaurs with giant claws.

1 → **THERIZINOSAURUS** → 70cm
2 → **MEGARAPTOR** → 40cm
3 → **BARYONYX** → 37cm
4 → **DEINOCHEIRUS** → 30cm
5 → **SEGNOSAURUS** → 32cm

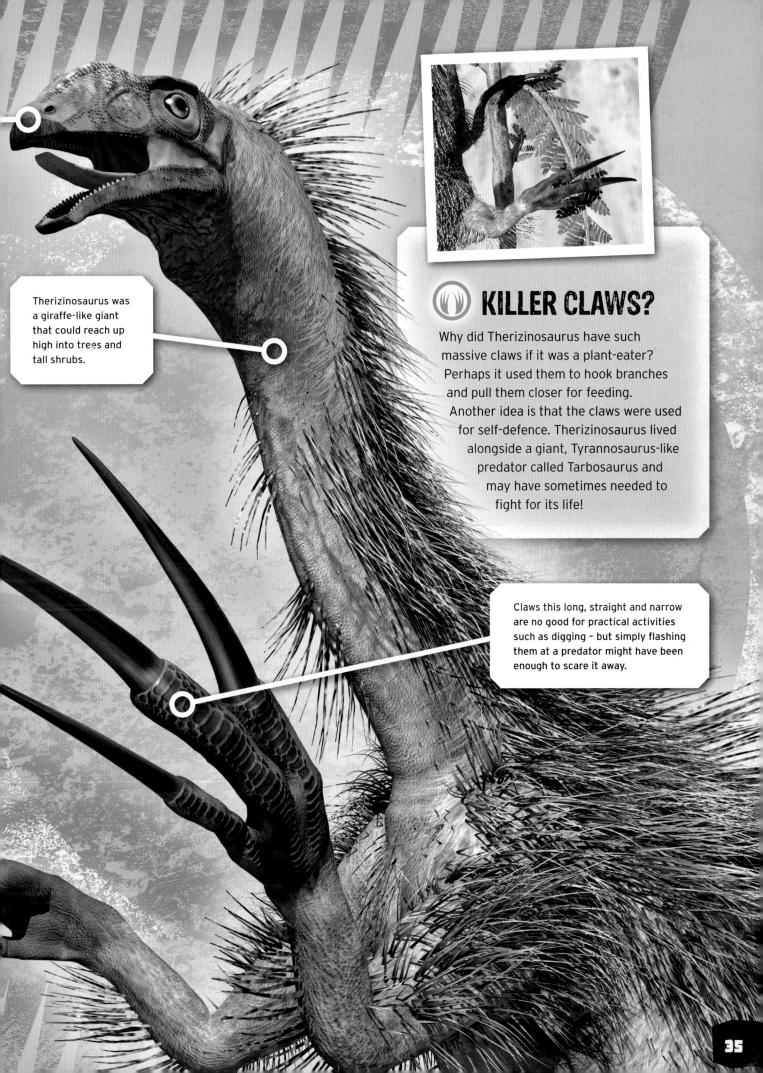

Therizinosaurus was a giraffe-like giant that could reach up high into trees and tall shrubs.

KILLER CLAWS?

Why did Therizinosaurus have such massive claws if it was a plant-eater? Perhaps it used them to hook branches and pull them closer for feeding. Another idea is that the claws were used for self-defence. Therizinosaurus lived alongside a giant, Tyrannosaurus-like predator called Tarbosaurus and may have sometimes needed to fight for its life!

Claws this long, straight and narrow are no good for practical activities such as digging – but simply flashing them at a predator might have been enough to scare it away.

TOUGHEST ARMOUR

ANKYLOSAURUS

Armoured dinosaurs such as Ankylosaurus were the tanks of the dinosaur world.

Their bodies bristled with armour plates, spikes and horns. The toughest, most heavily armoured of all was Ankylosaurus (an-ky-low-saw-rus). It probably chose not to run away from predators, but instead used its armour and tail club to fend them off.

The rounded shape of the armour plates may have helped to deflect the teeth of attacking predators.

🛡 BIG AS A BUS

Ankylosaurus was as heavy as a bus and nearly as long, with a wide, round body and short, thick limbs. This must have made it almost impossible to tip over! It had rows of armour plates along its back and tail and an armour-plated collar across its neck and shoulders. Even these defences may not have been enough to stop a Tyrannosaurus bite. Luckily Ankylosaurus also had large horns and a big tail club to fight with.

🛡 HAMMER TAIL

Ankylosaurus would probably aim to hit an attacking enemy on its head or legs with its tail club. The club was strong and heavy enough to break bone and was made from several large, bony plates locked together around the end of the tail. The bones in the tail were fused together to make a 'handle' to swing the club.

Ankylosaurus arm bones were thick and short. They helped the body to spin round quickly, so that the Ankylosaurus could strike an enemy with its tail.

🛡 BULLET PROOF

Ankylosaurus's armour was thin, but very strong. Some studies show that it was as strong as Kevlar, the material used to make bullet-proof vests. Of course, guns and bullets weren't around in the Cretaceous period, but big predators with powerful teeth and jaws like Tyrannosaurus rex sometimes attacked Ankylosaurus.

ANKYLOSAURUS
(an-ky-low-saw-rus)

WHEN	Cretaceous 65-70 mya
WHERE	USA
SIZE	7m long
WEIGHT	About 6 tonnes
DIET	Herbivorous
SPEED	Up to 24km/h
DANGER	MEDIUM

Ankylosaur defences included triangular horns sticking out from the sides and top of the head.

Ankylosaurus even had bony shutters to protect its eyes.

FASTEST TAIL!

DIPLODOCUS

Giant sauropods like Diplodocus (dip-lo-doe-cus) had amazing tails. The end was highly flexible, skinny, and shaped like a bullwhip.

Some scientists believe its tail was actually used like a whip and that the tip could be swished at supersonic speeds. If true, dinosaurs were the first living things in history to break through the sound barrier!

A few fossilised patches of skin show that sauropods were covered in small, rounded scales, though some kinds had armour plates and short bony lumps as well.

TOP TO TAIL

We now know that Diplodocus and its relatives had a row of tall, triangular spines running along the top of the neck, back and tail. This spiky fringe - similar to that of modern iguanas - would have given these dinosaurs a more showy appearance than previously imagined.

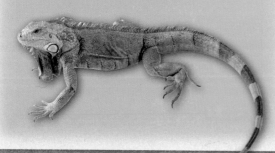

DIPLODOCUS
(dip-lo-doe-cus)

WHEN	Jurassic 150-147 mya
WHERE	USA
SIZE	32m long
WEIGHT	30 tonnes
DIET	Herbivorous
SPEED	Up to 16km/h
DANGER	HIGH

FASTER THAN SOUND?

Some experts think that the tail-tip of Diplodocus could have been used to make a loud 'crack' to scare other dinosaurs or to attract a mate. A whip makes this noise when its tip travels at more than 1,206 kilometres per hour. The whip's tip breaks through the sound barrier and makes a small sonic boom, just as an aircraft does when it reaches similar speeds.

Many dinosaurs had powerful tails, but Diplodocus was exceptional. Enormous bony 'wings' sticking out from the sides of the tail bones anchored massive muscles. These allowed the tail to be thrashed from side to side.

LIVING WHIP

If Diplodocus did use its tail tip as a whip to lash out at an attacker, it would have to be careful. Such heavy use could have snapped Diplodocus's tail or shredded it of its skin.

Sauropods like Diplodocus are usually imagined as 'gentle giants', but big modern plant-eaters such as rhinoceroses are often dangerous and aggressive. Diplodocus's giant size, powerful kick and enormous whiplash tail would have made it a formidable creature.

MOST MYSTERIOUS

DEINOCHEIRUS

In 1965, scientists collecting fossils in Mongolia's Gobi Desert found the remains of a dinosaur they named Deinocheirus (dine-oh-ky-rus).

So far only its hands, arms, shoulder blades and a few ribs have been discovered, so it has become famous for being mysterious!

? GIGANTIC GUESS

From the few bones we have, scientists have worked out that Deinocheirus was an enormous animal, similar in size to Tyrannosaurus rex. It may have had long, slender hind legs for fast running, a beaked jaw and enormous eyes – but these are all guesses. Experts would love to find other bones and to learn more about it.

? TOP 5 MYSTERY MONSTERS

The dinosaurs that experts would love to know more about!

1 → **DEINOCHEIRUS** → LONG-ARMED GIANT
2 → **AMPHICOELIAS** → GIANT SUPER-SAUROPOD
3 → **MEGARAPTOR** → BIG-CLAWED PREDATOR
4 → **YAVERLANDIA** → SMALL THICK-HEADED DINOSAUR
5 → **XENOPOSEIDON** → FREAKY-LOOKING SAUROPOD

DEINOCHEIRUS
(dine-oh-ky-rus)

WHEN	Cretaceous 65-70 mya
WHERE	Mongolia
SIZE	Up to 12m long
WEIGHT	Up to 6 tonnes
DIET	Probably omnivorous
SPEED	Up to 40km/h
DANGER	UNKNOWN

Deinocheirus may have been covered in hair-like feathers, like the small ostrich dinosaurs.

Its huge three-fingered hands were tipped with massive curved claws. These would have been good for hooking and pulling at branches.

? DEADLY KILLER?

When Deinocheirus was first discovered, experts thought it was a meat-eater that grabbed prey with its claws and ripped flesh with its sharp teeth. That's why it was given a fierce name meaning 'terrible hands'. However, we now know that its hand claws (below) were blunt and only slightly curved, so it is unlikely they were used for killing.

Healed injuries and rough patches on fossilised bones show that Deinocheirus used its hands a lot.

? SUPERLONG ARMS

Deinocheirus's arms were an amazing 2.5 metres in length – that's longer than a bath tub. They were long and straight, like those of ostrich-type dinosaurs such as Struthiomimus. This leads us to think that it was a gigantic member of this plant-eating group and not a hunter.

TOOTHIEST PREDATOR

PELECANIMIMUS

Record-breaking predator Pelecanimimus (pel-e-can-ee-mime-us) had about 220 teeth. That's over three times more than most meat-eating dinosaurs.

What makes Pelecanimimus especially remarkable is that it belongs to a group of dinosaurs that is famous among dinosaur experts for having no teeth!

The teeth at the tip of the upper jaw were shaped like a letter D in cross section. They may have been used for grabbing prey or for grooming.

Unlike most predators, Pelicanimimus's teeth are tiny and closely-spaced.

 MYSTERY MUNCHER

Only part of one Pelecanimimus skeleton has ever been found, so we don't know for certain why it had so many teeth. One idea is that they acted like the serrated edges of a pair of shears. This would have been useful for catching and slicing up small animals like lizards (below) and little birds. Its teeth may also have been used for filtering shrimps out of water.

TOP 5 TOOTHIEST PREDATORS

1 ➡ **PELECANIMIMUS** ➡ UP TO 220 TEETH
2 ➡ **BUITRERAPTOR** ➡ UP TO 140 TEETH
3 ➡ **BYRONOSAURUS** ➡ UP TO 128 TEETH
4 ➡ **SUCHOMIMUS** ➡ 122 TEETH
5 ➡ **BARYONYX** ➡ UP TO 112 TEETH

PELICAN MIMIC

The only Pelecanimimus specimen we have was found in beautiful condition and even had some of its original skin fossilised. Floppy folds of skin hung down from its lower jaw just like a modern-day pelican's pouch. This is where its name, meaning 'pelican mimic', comes from.

PELECANIMIMUS
(pel-e-can-ee-mime-us)

WHEN	Cretaceous 137-144 mya
WHERE	Spain
SIZE	2.5m long
WEIGHT	30kg
DIET	Possibly omnivorous
SPEED	Up to 48km/h
DANGER	LOW

The teeth further back in the jaw were peg-shaped and were probably used for slicing and cutting.

GONE FISHING

The upper and lower jaws of Pelecanimimus were long and shallow. Animals with jaws like this often feed by reaching into water and grabbing slippery prey, so perhaps Pelecanimimus mostly ate water animals.

BIGGEST SHOW OFF!

STEGOSAURUS

Stegosaurus (steg-oh-saw-rus) had some of the most impressive structures ever found on an animal's body. These were probably used for 'showing off'.

Enormous diamond-shaped plates more than 70 centimetres tall and 80 centimetres wide grew from its neck, back and tail. It's even possible that they were brightly-coloured.

 ## PUZZLING PLATES

Stegosaurus's plates weren't just made of bone. They also had a horny covering on top, but this has not survived in fossils. We know that this covering was living, growing material, but we don't know how big or what shape it was. These plates could have been even bigger than we imagine!

The plates stuck upwards and slightly outwards, so they would have been useless as body armour. Stegosaurus was about the size of a bus, so it probably relied on its size to defend itself.

PLAYING IT COOL?

Stegosaurus might have used its plates to control its body temperature. They could have absorbed the sun's heat to keep the dinosaur warm, or given off heat like a radiator, helping it to cool down when it was hot.

STEGOSAURUS
(steg-oh-saw-rus)

WHEN	Jurassic 145-155 mya
WHERE	USA, Portugal
SIZE	7m long
WEIGHT	3.5 tonnes
DIET	Herbivorous
SPEED	16km/h
DANGER	MEDIUM

Most similar dinosaurs had pairs of plates in a row, but Stegosaurus plates were arranged in an alternating pattern.

The plates on the neck were small. The biggest plates were over the hips and base of the tail.

FASHION STATEMENT

There were several species of dinosaurs similar to Stegosaurus, such as Loricatosaurus (below), but they had smaller plates in different shapes. Perhaps different types of stegosaur had different-shaped plates. This might have helped them to tell each other apart, so they could show off to their own kind.

LONGEST HEAD CREST

NYCTOSAURUS

Pterosaurs were flying reptiles that ruled the prehistoric skies and often had crested heads. The longest crest of all belonged to a pterosaur called Nyctosaurus (nik-tow-saw-rus) that soared over the seas.

It was a huge, Y-shaped crest, nearly four times as long as the rest of the skull. No other animal of the Mesozoic era grew a crest this large.

Most crested pterosaurs had flattened crests shaped like sheets or triangles. The incredible Nyctosaurus 'antler' was totally unique.

The crest was made of bone, but we don't know how heavy it was.

NYCTOSAURUS
(nik-tow-saw-rus)

WHEN	Cretaceous 85-84 mya
WHERE	USA
SIZE	2m wingspan
WEIGHT	2.6kg
DIET	Fish, marine molluscs
SPEED	24km/h
DANGER	NONE

 ### BIG HEADED

Nyctosaurus was not a large Pterosaur. At 2 metres, its wingspan was similar to that of a Bald Eagle, but its body was just 40 centimetres long. The crest was twice the length of its body and almost as long as a wing. For its body size, therefore, the crest was enormous.

TOP 3 BIGGEST CRESTS

1 → **NYCTOSAURUS** → CREST 4 X LONGER THAN SKULL
2 → **THALASSODROMEUS** → CREST 1.25 X LONGER THAN SKULL
3 → **PTERANODON** → CREST NEARLY SAME SIZE AS SKULL

1. Nyctosaurus   2. Thalassodromeus   3. Pteranodon

MALE OR FEMALE?

Until quite recently, all the Nyctosaurus fossils found had a short crest at the back of the head. When two new fossils with a long Y-shaped crest were discovered, it was thought that they belonged to a new species. But there is another explanation. It is now thought that the crestless fossils may be female, while the crested ones are male.

SAILING THE SKIES?

One theory suggests that the prongs of the crest were connected by a sheet of skin, which acted like the sail or rudder on a boat. To test this theory, scientists made some models of pterosaur heads and observed their behaviour against the force of the wind. The crests did not work well as sails or rudders, so the theory is unlikely to be true.

Nyctosaurus had small hind legs and long, slender wings. Because it hunted over the ocean, Nyctosaurus probably spent most of its time flying.

BIGGEST PREDATOR!

SPINOSAURUS

Spinosaurus (spine-oh-saw-rus) may have been the biggest two-legged predator that ever lived and was certainly one of the scariest-looking animals of all time.

Fossils found in North Africa show that it had a huge sail on its back and crocodile-like jaws. It was almost twice as long as a bus and weighed more than two fully-grown male elephants.

 ## FISH SUPPER

The narrow snout and lower jaws of Spinosaurus look similar to those of a modern-day crocodile. This makes it likely that Spinosaurus reached into water to grab fish, rather than killing other dinosaurs. It has been found in areas that were once tropical lagoons, where giant fish up to 3 metres long would have provided food.

 ## TOP 5 BIG KILLERS

These are the five biggest hunting dinosaurs found so far.

1 → **SPINOSAURUS**
2 → **GIGANOTOSAURUS**
3 → **TYRANNOSAURUS REX**
4 → **CARCHARODONTOSAURUS**
5 → **MAPUSAURUS**

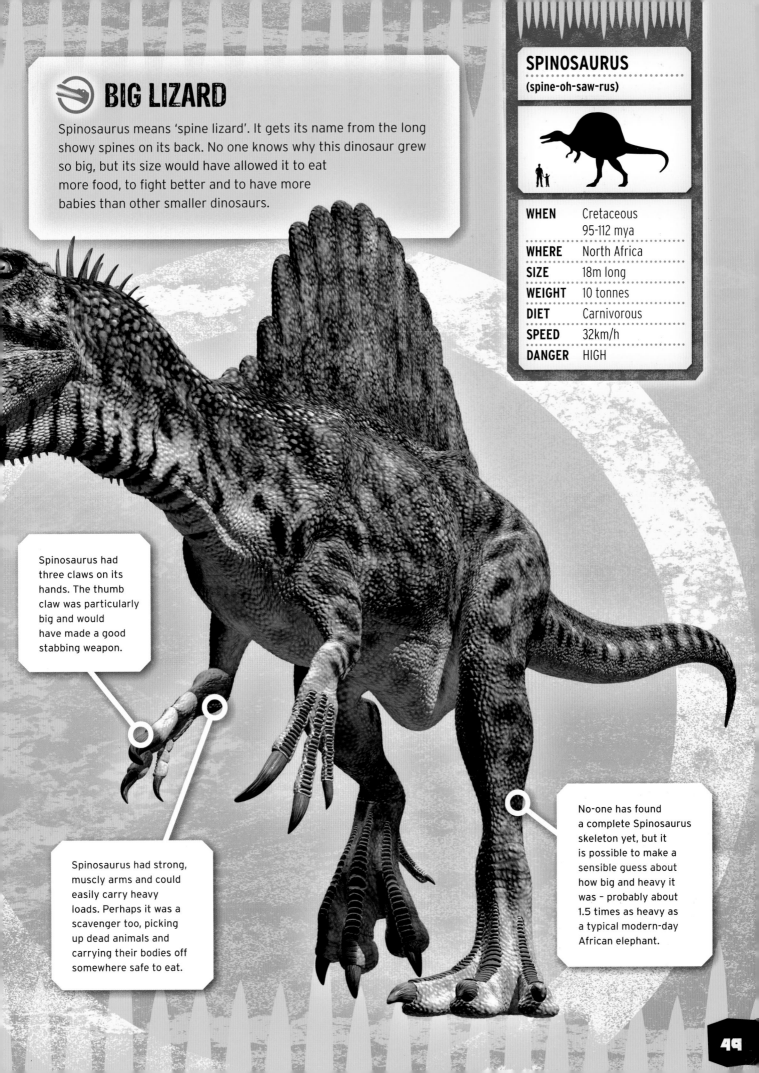

⊘ BIG LIZARD

Spinosaurus means 'spine lizard'. It gets its name from the long showy spines on its back. No one knows why this dinosaur grew so big, but its size would have allowed it to eat more food, to fight better and to have more babies than other smaller dinosaurs.

SPINOSAURUS
(spine-oh-saw-rus)

WHEN	Cretaceous 95-112 mya
WHERE	North Africa
SIZE	18m long
WEIGHT	10 tonnes
DIET	Carnivorous
SPEED	32km/h
DANGER	HIGH

Spinosaurus had three claws on its hands. The thumb claw was particularly big and would have made a good stabbing weapon.

Spinosaurus had strong, muscly arms and could easily carry heavy loads. Perhaps it was a scavenger too, picking up dead animals and carrying their bodies off somewhere safe to eat.

No-one has found a complete Spinosaurus skeleton yet, but it is possible to make a sensible guess about how big and heavy it was – probably about 1.5 times as heavy as a typical modern-day African elephant.

SMALLEST PLANT-EATER

FRUITADENS

The smallest plant-eater yet discovered is little Fruitadens (froot-ah-dens). A fully-grown adult was only about the size of a cat.

It ran on its back legs and used its teeth to mash up leaves and fruit. It might have used its claws to grab fruit and small lizards.

Small dinosaurs like Fruitadens had many predators. Its very long, flexible tail may have helped it to balance when running on its back legs, increasing the speed of its get-away.

SMALL IS SMART?

DISADVANTAGES OF BEING SMALL

★ BIG ANIMALS OR BAD WEATHER CAN EASILY DESTROY A SMALL DINOSAUR'S HOME

★ IT TAKES A LOT OF EFFORT TO MOVE LONG DISTANCES

★ SMALL DINOSAURS OFTEN HAVE TO EAT A LOT FOR THEIR SIZE

★ EVEN SMALL ANIMALS LIKE LIZARDS AND BIG SPIDERS MIGHT BE A THREAT

ADVANTAGES OF BEING SMALL

★ SMALL DINOSAURS CAN EASILY HIDE FROM PREDATORS AND BAD WEATHER

★ SMALL DINOSAURS ONLY NEED A SMALL LIVING SPACE TO SLEEP IN

★ SMALL DINOSAURS CAN GET ALL THE FOOD THEY NEED FROM JUST TWO OR THREE TREES

★ SMALL DINOSAURS CAN FEED ON EASY-TO-FIND FOODS LIKE SMALL BUGS AND SEEDS

FRUITADENS
(froot-ah-dens)

WHEN	Jurassic 150 mya
WHERE	USA
SIZE	70cm long
WEIGHT	About 800g
DIET	Herbivorous or omnivorous
SPEED	Up to 40km/h
DANGER	LOW

MODERN-DAY MINI DINOS

Birds evolved in the Jurassic period from small predatory dinosaurs, so it could be said that really small dinosaurs are still alive today! Perhaps we should keep them in mind when talking about the record for the smallest dinosaur! This tiny Cuban bee hummingbird, for example, is just 5 centimetres long.

Tiny dinosaurs like Fruitadens would need to hide from big predators. They might have slept in burrows.

Fruitaden's body and tail may have been covered in long, hair-like fibres.

FUNNY FANGS

Fruitadens belongs to a group of dinosaurs called the heterodontosaurs, which means 'different-toothed dinosaurs'. Their jaws had beaked tips, with teeth for chewing at the back. What makes them unusual is that they had fangs at the front, probably used for biting, fighting and showing off.

STRANGEST HEAD SHAPE

NIGERSAURUS

Nigersaurus (nee-zher-saw-rus), a small plant-eater that was found in Niger, West Africa, wins the prize for the dinosaur with the strangest head shape.

Its mouth was the widest part of its head, so it would have looked very odd – a bit like an old-fashioned vacuum cleaner. It could use its strange-shaped mouth to take extra-big bites of plant material.

MEGA MOUTH

Nigersaurus's wide mouth suggests that it fed at ground level on small plants, and could get large mouthfuls with every bite. This would make it a bit like some broad-mouthed mammals today, such as some modern rhinos. It had a short neck, so it probably reached downwards more than upwards.

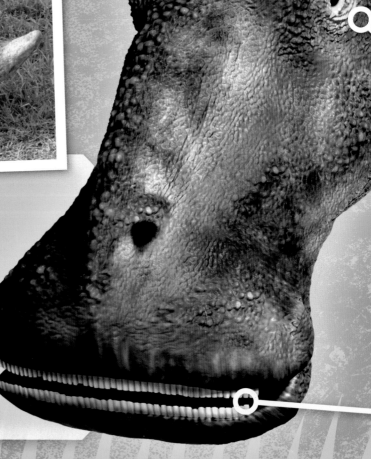

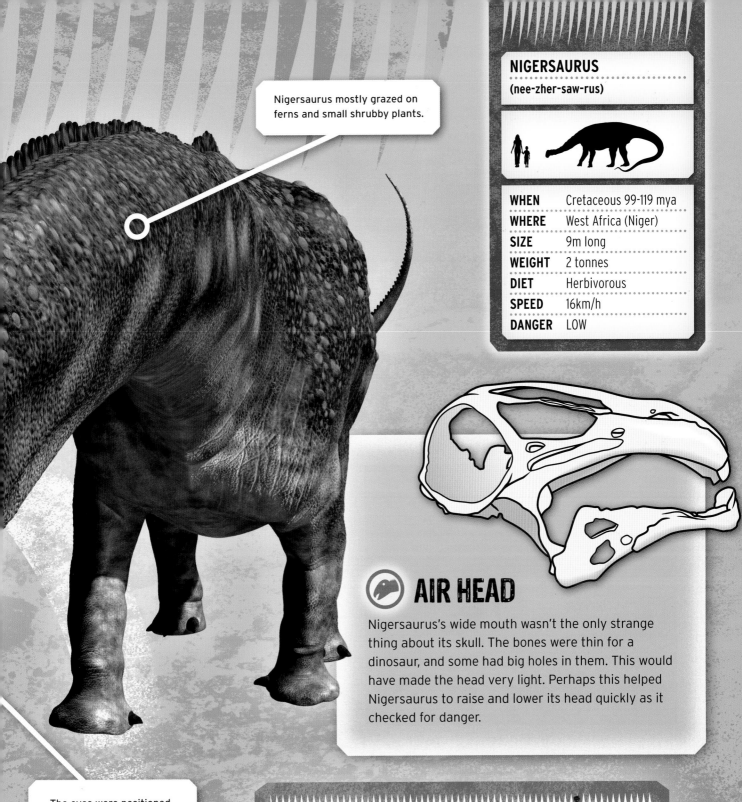

Nigersaurus mostly grazed on ferns and small shrubby plants.

NIGERSAURUS
(nee-zher-saw-rus)

WHEN	Cretaceous 99-119 mya
WHERE	West Africa (Niger)
SIZE	9m long
WEIGHT	2 tonnes
DIET	Herbivorous
SPEED	16km/h
DANGER	LOW

AIR HEAD

Nigersaurus's wide mouth wasn't the only strange thing about its skull. The bones were thin for a dinosaur, and some had big holes in them. This would have made the head very light. Perhaps this helped Nigersaurus to raise and lower its head quickly as it checked for danger.

The eyes were positioned far back on the sides of the head to provide good all-round vision.

CHEW ON THIS

Nigersaurus chewed its food with lots of small pencil-like teeth, but the tough plants it ate quickly wore these down. Rows of new teeth sat behind the ones being used, ready to replace them when they wore out. This meant Nigersaurus had more than 500 teeth in its mouth at any one time.

The muscles responsible for opening and closing the jaws were small, so Nigersaurus must have had a weak bite.

BEST PACK HUNTER

DEINONYCHUS

Fossil finds suggest that the bird-like predator Deinonychus (dine-oh-nye-kus) hunted in groups. Several have been found jumbled up with the remains of a large plant-eater, Tenontosaurus.

Because modern lizards, crocodiles and birds sometimes gang up to overpower or outsmart prey, it is likely that some dinosaurs did too. Maybe Deinonychus lived alone, and only ganged up when the opportunity arose. But it could have lived in family groups, working together.

Deinonychus was similar in size to a large wolf and was definitely capable of killing small dinosaurs on its own.

Deinonychus probably used its massive foot claws and curved hand claws to wound its prey. If Deinonychus managed to damage the windpipe and blood vessels of the victim's neck, the animal would weaken and almost certainly die.

Powerful leg muscles and strong bones suggest that Deinonychus probably leapt onto prey during an attack. Its arm and tail feathers could have helped to control the angle of the leap.

No one is sure exactly how Deinonychus killed prey, but its many curved, sharp teeth must have been good at slicing into flesh. They could also have been useful for tearing up prey into bite-size chunks.

DEINONYCHUS
(dine-oh-nye-kus)

WHEN	Cretaceous 115-108 mya
WHERE	USA
SIZE	3m long
WEIGHT	60kg
DIET	Carnivorous
SPEED	Up to 56km/h
DANGER	HIGH

An adult Tenontosaurus was a large and dangerous animal with a strong bite. Predators would have had to avoid sweeps of its enormous tail and powerful kicks from its legs.

Some predators that hunt in groups use tactics. While some individuals chase the prey, others might come in from the side to attack the neck or belly, for example.

LARGEST EGG

HYPSELOSAURUS

The largest dinosaur eggs found so far are the giant ball-shaped eggs belonging to Hypselosaurus (hip-sell-oh-saw-rus).

The largest ones were nearly 30 centimetres long, 25 centimetres wide and had a volume of about 3.3 litres. That's equivalent to about 73 chicken eggs!

EGG LAYING DINO-STYLE

Dinosaurs like Hypselosaurus didn't built complicated nests. Instead, they laid their eggs in lines or rough circles. Then they probably hid the eggs under sand or soil. We don't know if the parents stayed to guard the eggs, or if they left them to hatch on their own. Exactly what happened is a great unsolved mystery!

EGG RECORD BREAKER

Hypselosaurus takes the record for the largest dinosaur eggs, but the all-time record for the biggest eggs goes to a bird called Aepyornis from Madagascar. Nicknamed the 'elephant bird', this huge creature died out just a few hundred years ago. Its eggs were up to 39 centimetres long and 32 centimetres wide, with a volume equivalent to 4 Hypselosaurus eggs or about 292 chicken eggs!

Aepyornis Egg   Hypselosaurus Egg   Chicken Egg

HYPSELOSAURUS
(hip-sell-oh-saw-rus)

WHEN	Cretaceous 70-65 mya
WHERE	France
SIZE	15m long
WEIGHT	7 tonnes
DIET	Herbivorous
SPEED	16km/h
DANGER	MEDIUM

TOP 3 LARGEST DINOSAUR EGGS

1 ➡ **HYPSELOSAURUS**
   EQUIVALENT TO 73 CHICKEN EGGS

2 ➡ **MACROELONGATOOLITHUS**
   EQUIVALENT TO 70 CHICKEN EGGS

3 ➡ **HYPACROSAURUS**
   EQUIVALENT TO 65 CHICKEN EGGS

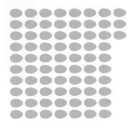

Chicken Eggs

Hypselosaurus Egg

Little is known about the body shape of Hypselosaurus, but we do know it was very big – perhaps up to 15 metres long.

WHO'S INSIDE?

When eggs become fossilised, it is usually only the shell that remains. It is very rare that the bones of the baby dinosaur inside are also preserved. When bones are found inside, however, it allows experts to identify which dinosaur laid the egg. So far, the remains of babies haven't been found inside any Hypselosaurus eggs.

These big claws could have been used to scrape up soil or sand to cover the freshly laid eggs.

When laying eggs, females probably squatted or laid down. This way the eggs wouldn't have to fall so far.

STRONGEST BITE!

The jaw bones of some predatory dinosaurs were flexible, allowing them to swallow big chunks of meat more easily. Tyrannosaurus rex's jaw bones were different. Some of the bones were fused together, making them stiff, but giving them an even stronger bite.

TYRANNOSAURUS REX

Tyrannosaurus rex (tie-ran-oh-sore-us rex) wasn't just huge – it also had one of the strongest bites in the whole history of life.

Scientists have worked out that its bite was up to six times stronger than that of an alligator. With jaws so powerful, Tyrannosaurus rex could crunch bones in half and even bite right through the heads and bodies of its prey.

GIANT JAWS

Fossil evidence shows Tyrannosaurus rex's monster jaws at work. A Triceratops fossil, found in Montana, had one of its brow horns bitten clean off by a Tyrannosaurus rex, while an Edmontosaurus, also from Montana, is preserved with a giant chunk taken out of its tail. Tyrannosaurus rex was the only giant predator living alongside Edmontosaurus, so it must have been the attacker!

TOP 5 BITES

The top 5 predatory dinosaurs with the strongest bite are all members of the tyrannosaur family.

1 ➡ **TYRANNOSAURUS REX**
2 ➡ **TARBOSAURUS**
3 ➡ **DASPLETOSAURUS**
4 ➡ **ALBERTOSAURUS**
5 ➡ **GORGOSAURUS**

The roof of Tyrannosaurus rex's mouth was hard and bony to help the skull keep its shape during biting. Thick bones along the middle of the snout carried the impact of the bite.

WHEN	Cretaceous 67-65 mya
WHERE	USA, Canada
SIZE	12m long
WEIGHT	about 6 tonnes
DIET	Carnivorous
SPEED	Up to 29km/h
DANGER	HIGH

Massive neck muscles not only helped to power its bite, but also allowed Tyrannosaurus rex to lift heavy prey and to pull hard when biting or tearing an animal apart.

FEARSOME FANGS!

Tyrannosaurus rex's teeth were shaped like bullets. They were rounded in cross-section, had long roots, and were incredibly strong. The largest were up to 40 centimetres long, including the root. Smaller teeth at the front of the jaws were shaped for nipping. Those at the back were short, but strongly curved, and were probably used to break bones.

SPIKIEST NECK

AMARGASAURUS

A huge plant-eating dinosaur called Amargasaurus (ah-marg-ah-saw-rus) wins the record for the spikiest neck.

It had pairs of long bony spines poking out from its neck. These spiky spines grew from just behind the back of the head and ran down the length of the neck. It's also possible that these two rows of spikes were joined together with skin to make two sail shapes.

 STRANGE SPINES

Armargasaurus had nine pairs of spines growing out of its vertebrae (neck bones). All animal vertebrae have bony bits that stick out, but no other creature has ever had such long strange-looking spines. They were about 50 centimetres long and were rounded at the tips.

Bony spines also stuck up along the back and tail. These were probably covered in muscle and skin.

TOP 5 SPIKIEST DINOSAURS

1 → **AMARGASAURUS** → SPIKES ON NECK
2 → **EDMONTONIA** → SPIKES ON NECK, SHOULDERS AND SIDE
3 → **KENTROSAURUS** → SPIKES ON BACK, SHOULDERS AND TAIL
4 → **SAUROPELTA** → SPIKES ON NECK AND SHOULDERS
5 → **LORICATOSAURUS** → SPIKES ON SHOULDERS AND TAIL

FLAUNT IT!

Amargasaurus might have used its spines to defend itself from predators, like a modern-day porcupine does. It is also possible that the spikes clattered together to make a frightening noise. If they were connected by skin to form sails, they might even have been used for signalling to other dinosaurs.

The longest spines were in the middle part of the neck. The spines near the head were shorter.

Maybe amargasaurs fought one another by lashing their strong, flexible necks from side to side.

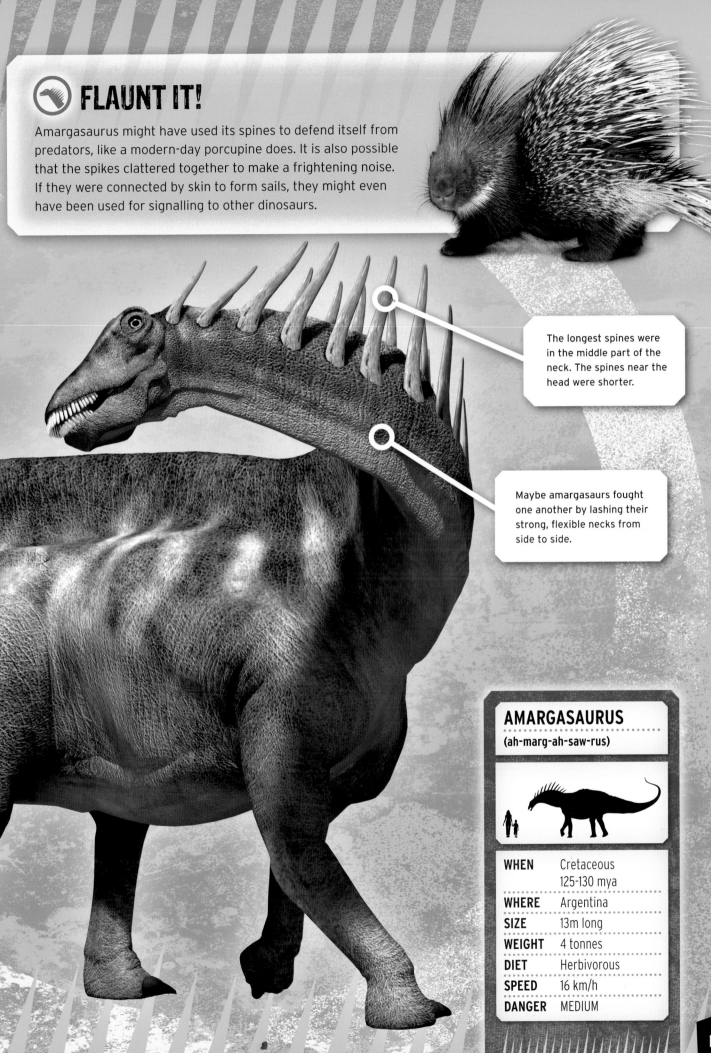

AMARGASAURUS
(ah-marg-ah-saw-rus)

WHEN	Cretaceous 125-130 mya
WHERE	Argentina
SIZE	13m long
WEIGHT	4 tonnes
DIET	Herbivorous
SPEED	16 km/h
DANGER	MEDIUM

HARDEST HEAD!

PACHYCEPHALOSAURUS

Hard-headed Pachycephalosaurus (pack-ee-seff-al-o-saw-rus) was a plant-eating dinosaur with a thick dome like a bowling ball on top of its head.

Its skull roof was an incredible 25 centimetres thick. By comparison, the top of your skull is only a few millimetres thick.

So far, only three Pachycephalosaurus skulls have been found. The lumps and bumps on each one are slightly different.

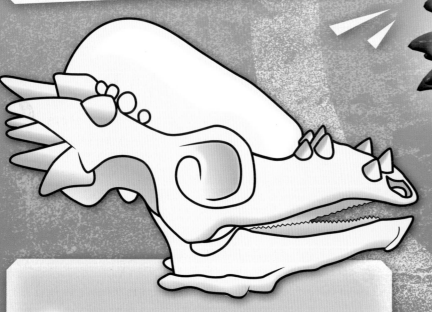

JUST FOR SHOW?

Bony lumps and spikes covered Pachycephalosaurus's snout and the back of its head. Some experts believe that these bumps may have made it look more attractive to mates and helped it to show off to other dinosaurs.

PACHYCEPHALOSAURUS
(pack-ee-seff-al-o-saw-rus)

WHEN	Cretaceous 70-65 mya
WHERE	USA
SIZE	5m long
WEIGHT	About 500kg
DIET	Omnivorous
SPEED	32 km/h
DANGER	LOW

TOUGH NUTS

Another theory is that these dinosaurs fought over mates or territory by smashing their heads together, or butting each other like American footballers. However, their skeletons don't seem strong enough to survive heavy blows, so the domes may have been just for show.

If Pachycephalosaurus used its dome for display, maybe it used its skin, too. Its skin might have had brightly coloured patches.

Pachycephalosaurus had small arms and hands and a long, stiffened tail. It could probably have run quite fast.

BABY BONEHEADS?

Some bonehead dinosaur fossils have smaller skull domes than Pachycephalosaurus, and some have no domes at all - just a flat skull roof with thorny spikes on top. Perhaps Pachycephalosaurus changed as it grew up and these domeless fossils are actually just younger individuals.

FIRST BIG DINOSAUR

HERRERASAURUS

The very first meat-eating dinosaur to evolve (develop) a really large body was Herrerasaurus (er-air-uh-saw-rus) from the Triassic period, about 230 million years ago.

It was nowhere near as big as the giant predatory dinosaurs that evolved later, but at 4.5 metres in length it was a giant compared to the dinosaurs that had lived before.

🦖 FACE OF A KILLER

Herrerasaurus had a huge, strong skull, a deep narrow snout and powerful jaws. About 80 serrated, blade-like teeth lined its jaws, some of them enormous. These features show that it could have attacked and killed very large animals – perhaps as big as itself. It probably weakened prey by taking slashing bites and causing blood loss. Once they were dead, it would have torn off big chunks of flesh for swallowing.

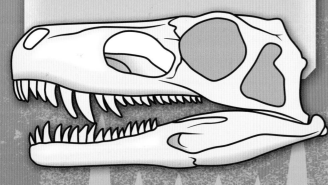

At 4.5 metres long, Herrerasaurus was huge. But later meat-eating dinosaurs would grow much, much larger: at least three times longer and as much as 50 times heavier!

CLUTCHING CLAWS

Herrerasaurus had three large, curved claws on long fingers. This suggests that it was one of the first dinosaurs to use its hands to grab and injure prey. Its palms faced inwards, so Herrerasaurus could only grab by bringing its hands together. It could have gripped prey while biting with its huge, sharp teeth.

WHEN	Triassic 230 mya
WHERE	Argentina
SIZE	4.5m long
WEIGHT	200kg
DIET	Carnivorous
SPEED	48km/h
DANGER	HIGH

Herrerasaurus had a shorter and less flexible neck than the later, more bird-like meat-eating dinosaurs of the Jurassic and Cretaceous periods.

DINOSAURS RULE

Early dinosaurs were small animals. They lived alongside a group of much larger, fierce crocodile-like reptiles known as crurotarsans (below). Herrerasaurus lived at the same time as these armour-plated monsters too, and probably avoided them whenever possible. Eventually, nearly all of the crurotarsans disappeared. Only then could dinosaurs begin to take over the planet.

Herrerasaurus lived more than 150 million years before more advanced predators like Tyrannosaurus rex. This means that there was more time between Herrerasaurus and Tyrannosaurus than there is between Tyrannosaurus and humans today!

GIANT-EYED SEA REPTILE

OPHTHALMOSAURUS

Ichthyosaurs were dolphin-shaped marine reptiles that roamed the prehistoric seas. One ichthyosaur called Ophthalmosaurus (off-thal-moe-saw-rus) had huge eyes compared to the size of its body.

Though this creature was only 4 metres long, its eyeballs were an incredible 23 centimetres in width - that's about the size of a melon. Huge eyes like this probably evolved so that Ophthalmosaurus could see and hunt prey in deep water.

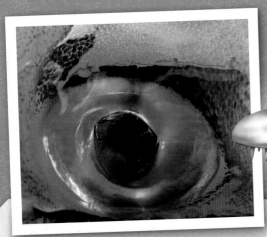

NIGHT VISION

Ophthalmosaurus's gigantic eyes suggest that it was able to see well in the dark. Like the eyes of modern-day giant squid (above), it is likely that they allowed it to travel hundreds of metres down to the dark zones of the ocean, looking for food.

One other ichthyosaur, Temnodontosaurus from England, had bigger eyes. However, it was a much bigger animal, so its eyes weren't as large compared to its body size.

Because eyes are filled with fluid, they don't change shape when an animal dives to great depth. The same is not true of the rest of the body. Organs become squashed and sometimes have to change position inside the body.

BIGGEST OCEAN EYES

Compare the size of Opthalmosaurus's eyes with two modern-day monsters of the deep.

1 ➡ **GIANT SQUID** ➡ 25cm WIDE
2 ➡ **OPHTHALMOSAURUS** ➡ 23cm WIDE
3 ➡ **BLUE WHALE** ➡ 15cm WIDE

Blue Whale   Ophthalmosaurus   Giant Squid

ALL IN THE EYES

We know Ophthalmosaurus had big eyes because the eye sockets in its skull (below) are huge – but we don't what shape its pupils were. Perhaps they were slit-shaped like some modern creatures with good night vision, such as cats. It's even possible they could have been square, like the pupils of some deep-diving penguins. Whatever shape they were, they would have got much bigger to let in light when Ophthalmosaurus was diving in deep, dark water.

Ophthalmosaurus was a speedy, tuna-shaped predator. It had a powerful tail to propel it through the water.

OPHTHALMOSAURUS
(off-thal-moe-saw-rus)

WHEN	Jurassic 165-145 mya
WHERE	All around world
SIZE	4m long
WEIGHT	1 tonne
DIET	Fish, squid
SPEED	9km/h
DANGER	MEDIUM

WORLDWIDE

Great eyesight helped to make Ophthalmosaurus a formidable hunter and to take advantage of the world's largest natural habitat – the ocean. That is why fossils of Ophthalmosaurus have been discovered worldwide, in areas that were covered by shallow seas during the Jurassic period.

LONGEST TAIL

LEAELLYNASAURA

The record for the longest tail compared to the size of its body belongs to a small, two-legged dinosaur called Leaellynasaura (lee-ally-nah-saw-rah).

Its tail had over 70 bones and was more than three times longer than its head, neck and body put together. That's the longest tail, compared to body length, of any dinosaur yet discovered.

Its long tail could have been used for balance when running and for signalling to others of its own kind.

Its skull shows that it had very large eyes, so it was probably good at finding food in the dark.

 WHY SO LONG?

Leaellynasaura is from southern Australia, which was inside the Antarctic Circle during the Cretaceous period. It would have been too small to migrate (travel long distances away from the cold), so it would have had to cope with months of freezing winter darkness. Its long tail could have acted as an energy store to help it through those long, dark days.

LEAELLYNASAURA
(lee-ally-nah-saw-rah)

WHEN	Cretaceous 125-120 mya
WHERE	Australia
SIZE	3m long
WEIGHT	90kg
DIET	Herbivorous
SPEED	48km/h
DANGER	NONE

LONGEST TAIL EVER!

Leaellynasaurus holds the record for the longest tail compared to body size, but the longest dinosaur tail ever belonged to a super-giant sauropod named Amphicoelias fragillimus.
We only have bits of its tail, but experts have worked out that it may have been over 30 metres long – that's about as long as three buses!

Other dinosaurs had a similar number of bones in their tails, but their bones were not long as those of Leaellynasaura.

SCARF TAIL

Leaellynasaura might have wrapped its super-long, flexible tail around itself to keep warm, like some modern-day animals such as snow leopards. Recent discoveries have shown that small plant-eating dinosaurs had hair-like fibres on their tails. If Leaellynasaura's tail was furry, this would have helped to keep it warm too.

DINOSAUR HIDEOUT

Leaellynasaura may have sheltered underground during the cold winter months. We already know that some small, two-legged dinosaurs were good diggers and made their home inside burrows, so it is possible that the fossilised burrows found near Leaellynasaura were made by this little dinosaur.

MOST IMPORTANT DISCOVERY

DEINONYCHUS

In 1964, a new bird-like dinosaur named Deinonychus (dine-oh-nye-kus), was discovered. It was the most important dinosaur find ever because it changed the way we think about dinosaurs.

The find showed that dinosaurs were not necessarily slow-moving lizard-like creatures, as many experts had thought. Instead some could move fast and even had warm-blooded, feathery, bird-like bodies.

Bird-like dinosaurs such as Deinonychus were once shown with scaly skin. New fossils have shown that, like birds, they were covered in feathers.

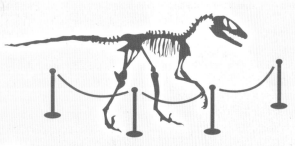

🖼 STARTING SOMETHING

The discovery of Deinonychus started a whole new wave of research – a scientific event known as the 'dinosaur renaissance'. It made scientists think again about what they knew about dinosaurs and led to many exciting exhibitions in museums. For this reason, Deinonychus can be regarded as the most important dinosaur find so far.

🦖 BIRD MAN

The scientist behind the discovery and study of Deinonychus was called John Ostrom (left). He is often described as the 'father' of the dinosaur renaissance because he was the first to realise that Deinonychus (right) and its relatives were closely related to birds and that birds had evolved from dinosaurs during the Jurassic period.

🦖 WARM OR COLD?

If Deinonychus was a fast moving bird-like creature, could it have been 'warm-blooded' like a modern bird, rather than 'cold-blooded' like a lizard? Ostrom thought that this was likely. One of his students, Robert Bakker (left), went on to suggest that all dinosaurs were active, warm-blooded animals. Others disagreed and arguments still go on today. It's possible that there were dinosaurs in both groups.

Deinonychus must have had big muscles powered by a big heart. These large muscles and organs might be evidence that dinosaurs like this were warm-blooded.

Deinonychus had its main weapons – its huge claws – on its feet. This meant that it would have had to be good at balancing in order to use them.

DEINONYCHUS
(dine-oh-nye-kus)

WHEN	Cretaceous 115-108 mya
WHERE	USA
SIZE	3m long
WEIGHT	60kg
DIET	Carnivorous
SPEED	Up to 56km/h
DANGER	HIGH

OLDEST BIRD

ARCHAEOPTERYX

Fossils show us that birds evolved (developed) from small predatory dinosaurs – and since birds still exist today, we can say that dinosaurs are not extinct!

The oldest bird we know of is Archaeopteryx (ar-kee-op-ter-rix). Though it could probably fly and was covered in feathers, it was extremely similar to other small, feathered predatory dinosaurs and must have evolved from them.

EARLY BIRD

Archaeopteryx would have looked very different from modern birds. In fact, it probably looked more like a small version of feathery meat-eating dinosaurs such as Velociraptor. Its narrow jaws were lined with tiny teeth (left). It had long clawed fingers, a long feathered tail and a deep narrow body.

ARCHAEOPTERYX
(ar-kee-op-ter-rix)

WHEN	Jurassic 150-155 mya
WHERE	Germany
SIZE	50cm long
WEIGHT	500g
DIET	Carnivorous
SPEED	48km/h
DANGER	NONE

BORN TO RUN

Because Archaeopteryx has always been imagined as the 'first bird', it is often shown as a perching animal, similar in shape to a pigeon. In fact, its long hind legs and the shape of its toes and toe claws suggest that it ran quickly on the ground, with the second toes of its feet raised up off the ground. Perhaps it only flew when planning to cover large distances or when escaping from danger.

Fossils show that Archaeopteryx had big feathers on its arms and tail. Some experts think it also had long feathers on its hind legs, but this is harder to prove.

★ ★ ★ ★ **KEY DIFFERENCES FROM MODERN BIRDS** ★ ★ ★ ★

MODERN BIRD | ARCHAEOPTERYX

VERSUS

★ **TOOTHLESS BEAK**	★ **TOOTHED JAWS**
★ FINGERS FUSED TOGETHER AND NO CLAWS OR SMALL CLAWS	★ LONG, SEPARATE FINGERS WITH BIG CLAWS
★ SHORT, STUBBY TAIL SKELETON	★ LONG, BONY TAIL SKELETON
★ SHALLOW, WIDE BODY SHAPE WITH VERY WIDE HIPS	★ DEEP, NARROW BODY SHAPE WITH NARROW HIPS
★ FIRST TOE ON FOOT OFTEN BIG AND POINTING BACKWARDS	★ FIRST TOE ON FOOT NOT FULLY TURNED BACKWARDS

Archaeopteryx probably had horny beak tissue around the edges of its jaws. But, unlike modern birds, it also had small teeth.

THE SURVIVORS

Archaeopteryx and other birds are dinosaurs. What makes birds different from other dinosaur groups is that they were the only group to survive the mass extinction that happened at the end of the Cretaceous, 65 million years ago. They probably survived because of their small size and ability to fly long distances.

Archaeopteryx lived on islands surrounded by a warm, shallow sea and might even have searched at the water's edge for dead fish and other prey.

TALLEST EVER!

SAUROPOSEIDON

Giant size, long front legs and a neck like a ship's mast makes plant-eater Sauroposeidon (saw-row-pa-side-un) the tallest dinosaur ever discovered.

At around 20 metres high, it could have looked into the windows of a six-storey building! Its neck was at least 11.5 metres long – perhaps longer.

The skull of Sauroposeidon has yet to be found. It may have looked similar to a dinosaur called Giraffatitan, which had a tall crest over the eyes.

SAUROPOSEIDON
(saw-row-pa-side-un)

WHEN	Cretaceous 115-105 mya
WHERE	USA
SIZE	27m long
WEIGHT	40 tonnes
DIET	Herbivorous
SPEED	16km/h
DANGER	HIGH

 GIANT GUESS?

Only a few neck bones of this dinosaur have been found – and some giant footprints (above) which probably belong to it, too – so we don't know for sure if Sauroposeidon was very tall rather than very long. However, nearly all modern-day land animals hold their necks upright, so it is thought that Sauroposeidon did too.

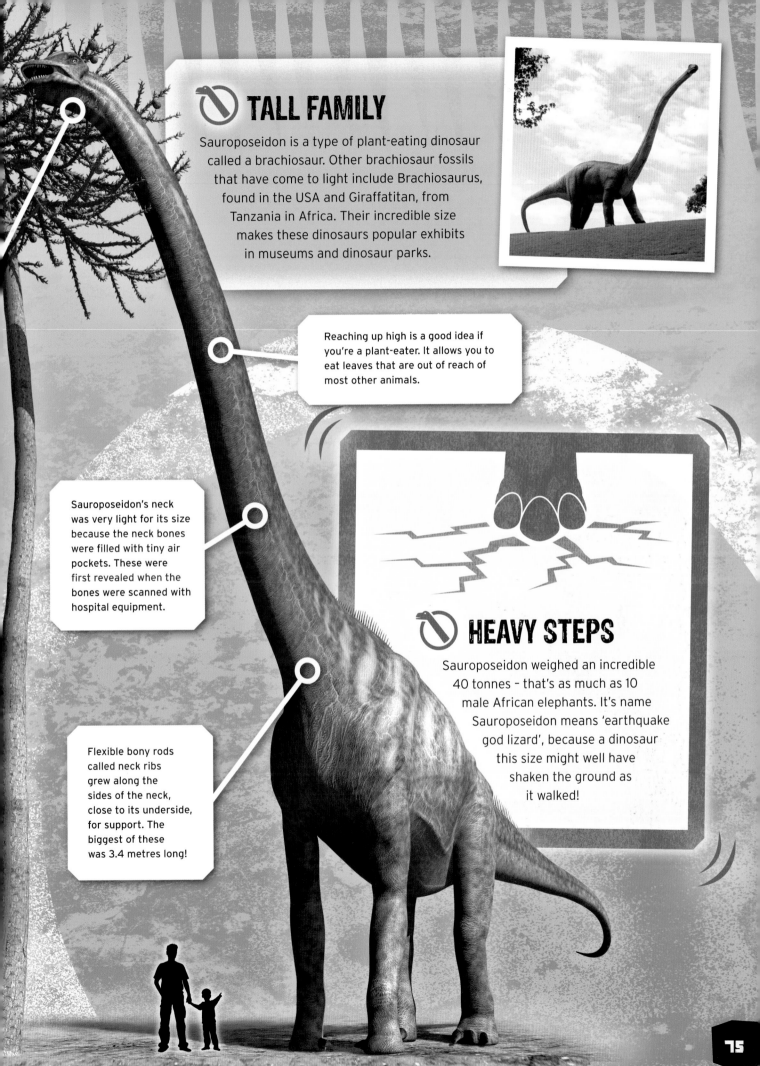

TALL FAMILY

Sauroposeidon is a type of plant-eating dinosaur called a brachiosaur. Other brachiosaur fossils that have come to light include Brachiosaurus, found in the USA and Giraffatitan, from Tanzania in Africa. Their incredible size makes these dinosaurs popular exhibits in museums and dinosaur parks.

Reaching up high is a good idea if you're a plant-eater. It allows you to eat leaves that are out of reach of most other animals.

Sauroposeidon's neck was very light for its size because the neck bones were filled with tiny air pockets. These were first revealed when the bones were scanned with hospital equipment.

HEAVY STEPS

Sauroposeidon weighed an incredible 40 tonnes – that's as much as 10 male African elephants. It's name Sauroposeidon means 'earthquake god lizard', because a dinosaur this size might well have shaken the ground as it walked!

Flexible bony rods called neck ribs grew along the sides of the neck, close to its underside, for support. The biggest of these was 3.4 metres long!

FUZZIEST DINOSAUR

PSITTACOSAURUS

One species of the small parrot-headed dinosaur Psittacosaurus (sitt-ack-uh-saw-rus) had long, fuzzy, feathery quills sticking up from its tail, making it the fuzziest dinosaur on record.

Experts are still trying to work out what the quills were for.

QUILL QUESTION

Psittacosaurus is one of the best known dinosaurs because hundreds of specimens have been discovered - but so far only one has been found with tail quills, though more may turn up eventually. It's possible that many of Psittacosaurus's relatives had tail quills too - perhaps even the big horned dinosaurs like Triceratops.

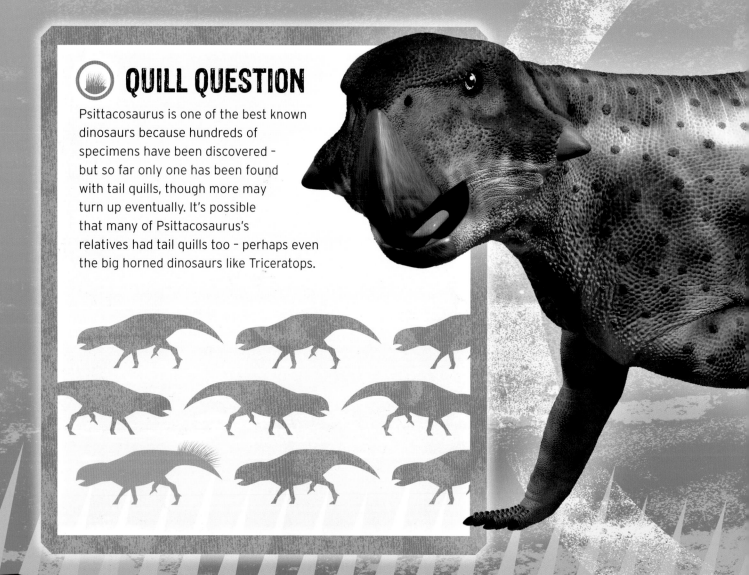

HEADS OR TAILS?

It seems that at least some Psittacosaurus had quills on their tails, but did they have them anywhere else on their bodies? When patches of Psittacosaurus skin are found they are always scaly rather than 'quilly', so probably not. It does seem, however, that some other small plant-eating dinosaurs had quills. Another dinosaur called Tianyulong from China also had some on its tail and may have had them all over its body.

WHEN	Cretaceous 105-115 mya
WHERE	Mongolia
SIZE	1m long
WEIGHT	About 6kg
DIET	Herbivorous
SPEED	Up to 40km/h
DANGER	LOW

The quills might have been brightly-coloured and used in display.

The quills were up to 16 centimetres long and round in cross-section. There were about 100 of them.

CAMOUFLAGE?

Some modern creatures such as sea dragons (right) use soft, feathery growths on their body to help them hide among plants. Perhaps Psittacosaurus used its long feathery quills in a similar way, breaking up its body shape when it hid in reeds and bushes. It is unlikely that Psittacosaurus used its fuzzy quills for protection because they were too soft and floppy.

LONGEST HORNS

WHEN	Cretaceous 72-70 mya
WHERE	Mexico
SIZE	7m long
WEIGHT	About 5 tonnes
DIET	Herbivorous
SPEED	32km/h
DANGER	MEDIUM

COAHUILACERATOPS

Coahuilaceratops (coh-whe-lah-serra-tops) was a horned plant-eater, with a small nose horn and two huge brow horns – probably the biggest ever!

At around one metre in length, each brow horn was nearly as long as a broom handle and would have given this plant-eater a terrifying appearance.

The edges of the frill were usually decorated with triangular bony lumps.

HEAD TO HEAD

It is likely that horned dinosaurs used their horns as weapons to fight among themselves, as well as to fend off predators. Some horned dinosaur fossils have been found with healed wounds on the skull and frill. These were probably made by the horns of opponents, which suggests that they fought one another for mates.

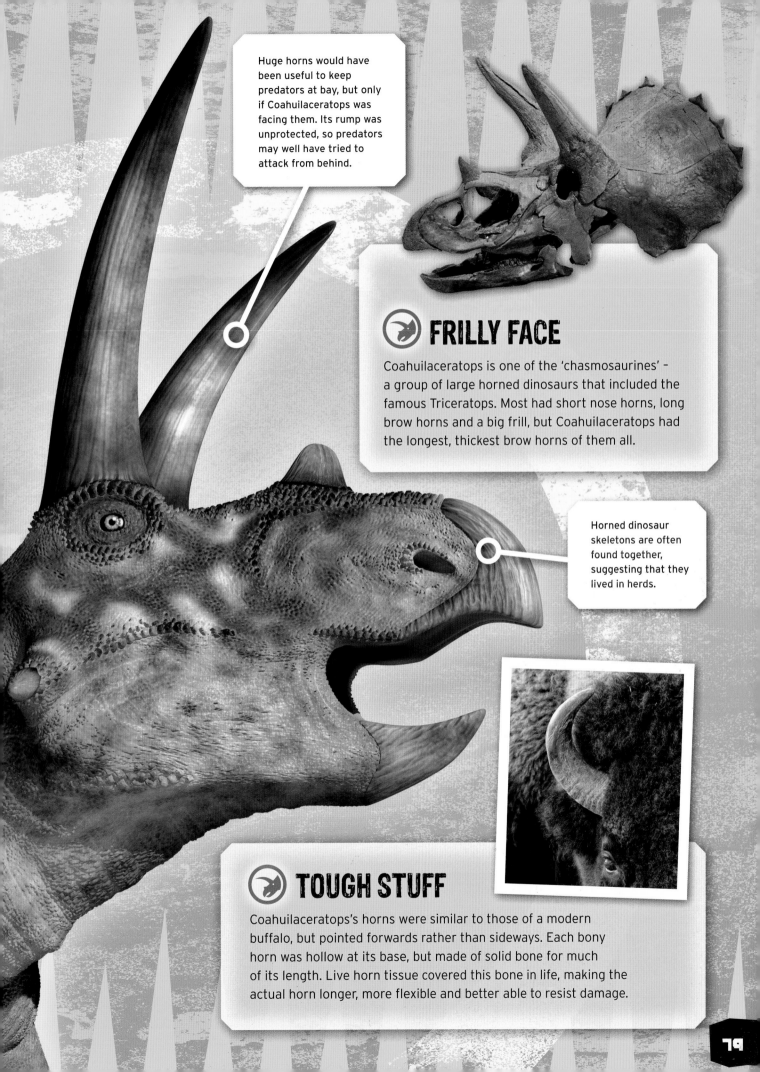

Huge horns would have been useful to keep predators at bay, but only if Coahuilaceratops was facing them. Its rump was unprotected, so predators may well have tried to attack from behind.

🦕 FRILLY FACE

Coahuilaceratops is one of the 'chasmosaurines' – a group of large horned dinosaurs that included the famous Triceratops. Most had short nose horns, long brow horns and a big frill, but Coahuilaceratops had the longest, thickest brow horns of them all.

Horned dinosaur skeletons are often found together, suggesting that they lived in herds.

🦕 TOUGH STUFF

Coahuilaceratops's horns were similar to those of a modern buffalo, but pointed forwards rather than sideways. Each bony horn was hollow at its base, but made of solid bone for much of its length. Live horn tissue covered this bone in life, making the actual horn longer, more flexible and better able to resist damage.

BRAINIEST DINOSAUR

TROODON

Agile, bird-like predator Troodon (troo-uh-don) boasts the title of 'brainiest dinosaur'.

Its brain was similar in size to that of an ostrich – about as big as a satsuma. That's not so big in the modern animal kingdom, but it is definitely big for a dinosaur.

 ## BRAIN POWER

Big brains are quite rare in the animal world because it takes a lot of energy to power them. One of their main advantages is that they allow animals to be better at communicating with each other and better at remembering the features of the world around them. For its body size, Troodon had the biggest brain of any dinosaur.

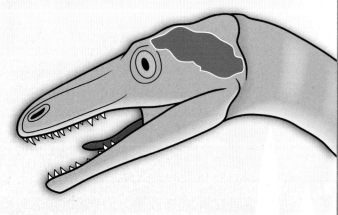

The brains of dinosaurs are usually found in a small space at the top and back of the skull. In contrast, human brains take up most of the space inside the skull.

Human-sized Troodon was probably a flexible hunter, smart enough to recognise all kinds of different objects as food. It could have eaten small animals, insects and even eggs and fruit.

Like other bird-like dinosaurs, Troodon was agile, speedy and had a good sense of balance. All of this was thanks to its big brain.

TROODON
(troo-uh-don)

WHEN	Cretaceous 70-65 mya
WHERE	USA, Canada
SIZE	2.5m long
WEIGHT	35kg
DIET	Omnivorous
SPEED	Up to 48km/h
DANGER	MEDIUM

SUPER SENSES

The sharper a predator's senses, the better it will be at hunting down prey. Most of Troodon's brain power was used for its senses, particularly sight and hearing. This helped to make it a highly successful hunter.

HOW CLEVER?

Troodon may have the biggest dinosaur brain, but compared to modern-day animals its brain was small. Some birds today have far bigger brains than Troodon and are much cleverer. The brainiest birds are parrots. Compared to body size, their brains are as big as those of monkeys and apes and some of them are similar in intelligence to human children! Troodon, however, was actually about as clever as a chicken or an ostrich.

LONGEST SPIKES

LORICATOSAURUS

Ferocious spikes more than a metre long sprouted from the tail of Loricatosaurus (lor-ee-cart-oh-saw-rus).

These are the longest spikes ever grown by any animal and were probably used to fight off enemies and impress mates.

⊛ SPIKY MYSTERY

When Loricatosaurus was alive, its spikes were even longer than the fossils that have been found - perhaps up to twice as long. This is because, like sheep's horns (below), the spikes weren't just made from bone, but were covered by a tough, horny sheath. This sheath was continually growing, but it does not survive in fossils, so we don't know how long it grew.

It's not clear exactly where all the spikes were on the body of Loricatosaurus. There may have been some on the shoulders or hips too.

⚘ BONY BACK

Dinosaurs such as Loricatosaurus had big plates sticking out of their backs, as well as tail spikes. Different types of stegosaur have been found with different-shaped plates and different numbers of spikes. Stegosaurus (above) had enormous diamond-shaped plates and four tail spikes. Other stegosaurs had smaller plates and more spikes.

LORICATOSAURUS
(lor-ee-cart-oh-saw-rus)

WHEN	Jurassic 160-164 mya
WHERE	England
SIZE	6m long
WEIGHT	2 tonnes
DIET	Herbivorous
SPEED	Up to 16km/h
DANGER	MEDIUM

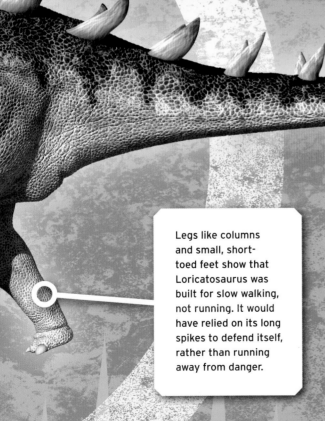

The longest spikes may have been on the end of Loricatosaurus's powerful tail. It probably walked with its tail sticking out.

Legs like columns and small, short-toed feet show that Loricatosaurus was built for slow walking, not running. It would have relied on its long spikes to defend itself, rather than running away from danger.

⚘ WATCH THAT TAIL

Loricatosaurus probably swung its tail spikes from side to side to pierce an attacker's flesh. A tail bone from an Allosaurus (a large, predatory dinosaur) was found with a hole made by a stegosaur tail spike. Fossilised tail spikes have also been found with damage marks on them. These marks are thought to have been caused by striking hard objects.

DEADLIEST DUEL!

The most spectacular evidence of combat between plant-eating and meat-eating dinosaurs comes from 'the fighting dinosaurs': a fossil of a Velociraptor and a Protoceratops that died while locked in battle.

Found in Mongolia in 1971, it is one of the most amazing dinosaur discoveries of all time.

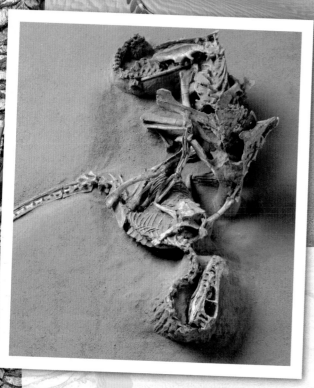

The fossil shows Protoceratops standing up, as if trying to pull away from Velociraptor and biting down hard on the predator's arm.

MORTAL COMBAT

Did this battling duo die at the same time from their injuries and stay locked together even after death? Maybe they were buried by a collapsing sand dune as they fought. It is also possible that they were suffocated by a raging sand storm.

VELOCIRAPTOR
(vel-oh-see-rap-tor)

WHEN	Cretaceous 71-75 mya
WHERE	Mongolia, China
SIZE	2.5m long
WEIGHT	25kg
DIET	Carnivorous
SPEED	24km/h
DANGER	HIGH

'The fighting dinosaurs' fossil helps us to understand how Velociraptor may have used the huge, curved sickle claws on its feet. Its left foot is close to Protoceratops's neck and the claw on that foot is raised up, as if stabbing into the blood vessels of the neck. Maybe sickle claws were used as vicious weapons for stabbing.

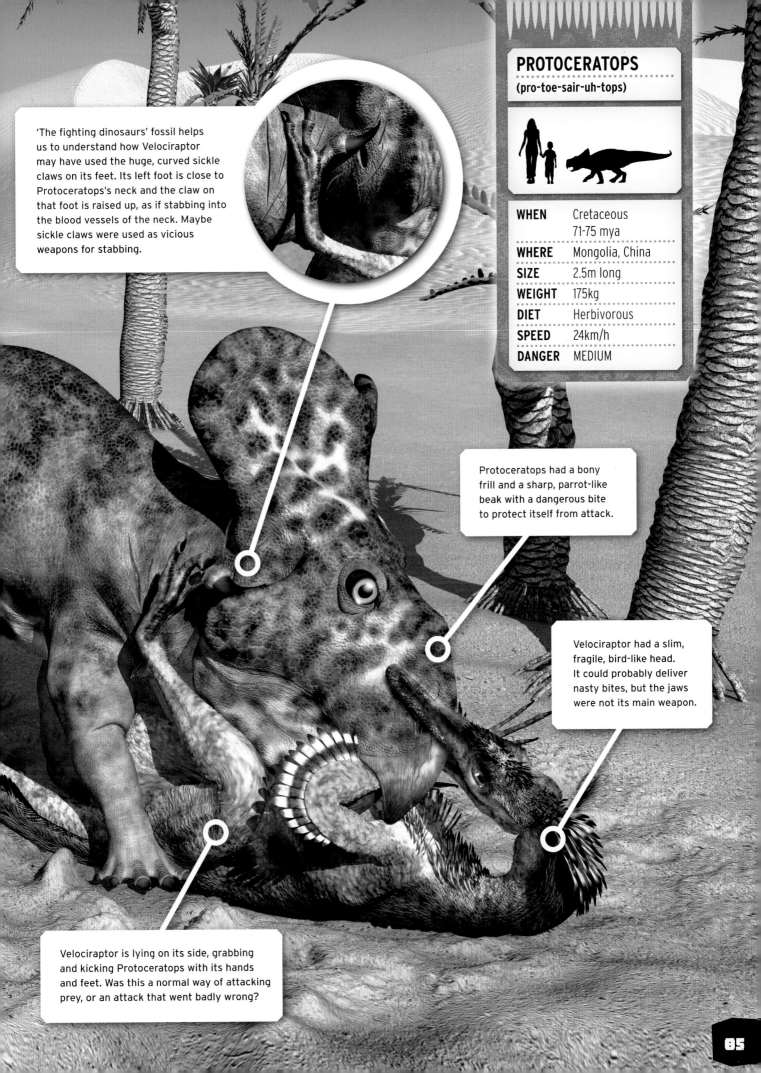

PROTOCERATOPS
(pro-toe-sair-uh-tops)

WHEN	Cretaceous 71-75 mya
WHERE	Mongolia, China
SIZE	2.5m long
WEIGHT	175kg
DIET	Herbivorous
SPEED	24km/h
DANGER	MEDIUM

Protoceratops had a bony frill and a sharp, parrot-like beak with a dangerous bite to protect itself from attack.

Velociraptor had a slim, fragile, bird-like head. It could probably deliver nasty bites, but the jaws were not its main weapon.

Velociraptor is lying on its side, grabbing and kicking Protoceratops with its hands and feet. Was this a normal way of attacking prey, or an attack that went badly wrong?

LONGEST NECK

OMEISAURUS

Omeisaurus (oh-may-saw-rus) holds the record for the longest neck of any dinosaur, compared to its body size.

A modern-day giraffe's neck is about twice as long as its body, but this dinosaur's neck was nearly 8.5 metres long. That's four times longer than its body.

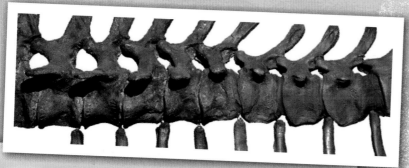

The neck of Omeisaurus was so long compared to its body and tail that it seems surprising it didn't topple forwards.

 LOADS OF BONES

Why did Omeisaurus have such a long neck? The answer lies in its skeleton. We have just seven bones, called vertebrae, in our necks. Most early dinosaurs had nine, but Omeisaurus had an impressive 17, which were also very long. Where other dinosaurs had back vertebrae, Omeisaurus had extra neck vertebrae, so its back was shorter and its neck was longer.

Omeisaurus had a big bony club at the tip of its tail. Perhaps it used this to whack approaching predators.

Its long, skinny neck must have lost a lot of heat. It would also make Omeisaurus an easy target for big predators.

GIRAFFE-STYLE

Just like modern-day giraffes, Omeisaurus used its incredible bendy neck to reach up into tall trees for food. It could also move its neck a long way to either side and reach down to the ground, so it could pick and choose from lots of different plants.

Long necks are great for reaching up high and looking around, but swallowing and pumping blood up to the head and brain are more of a problem. Omeisaurus must have adapted to cope with these problems, but we don't yet know how.

LONG NECK LEAGUE TABLE

Omeisaurus takes the record for the longest neck compared to its body size, but other dinosaurs had longer necks.

1 ➡ SUPERSAURUS ➡ 16 METRES LONG

2 ➡ MAMENCHISAURUS ➡ 12 METRES LONG

3 ➡ SAUROPOSEIDON ➡ AT LEAST 11.5 METRES LONG

4 ➡ OMEISAURUS ➡ 8.5 METRES LONG

OMEISAURUS
(oh-may-saw-rus)

WHEN	Jurassic 160-164 mya
WHERE	China
SIZE	18m long
WEIGHT	8.5 tonnes
DIET	Herbivorous
SPEED	16km/h
DANGER	LOW

BIGGEST FLYING ANIMAL...EVER!

QUETZALCOATLUS

Gigantic pterosaur Quetzalcoatlus (ket-zel-kwat-lus) holds the record for being not only the biggest flying reptile, but also the biggest flying animal ever.

It had a wingspan of 11 metres - about the same as a World War II Spitfire. For its size, though, Quetzalcoatlus was in fact extremely light: it was about the same weight as four men.

 ## WHOPPING WINGSPAN

Before Quetzalcoatlus was discovered, people thought that Pteranodon - with a maximum wingspan of 7 metres - was the biggest ever flier. The biggest flying bird today is called the wandering albatross. Its wingspan can sometimes reach up to 3.5 metres.

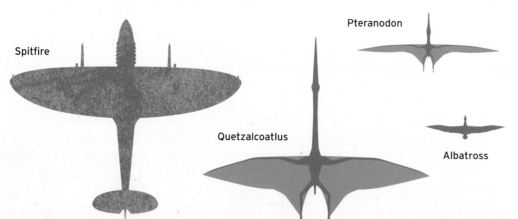

Spitfire

Pteranodon

Quetzalcoatlus

Albatross

QUETZALCOATLUS
(ket-zel-kwat-lus)

WHEN	Cretaceous 70-65 mya
WHERE	USA, Canada
SIZE	11m wingspan
WEIGHT	250kg
DIET	Omnivorous
SPEED	36km/h
DANGER	HIGH

SUPER FLAPPERS

Quetzalcoatlus had broad wings, similar in shape to modern storks and vultures. These birds soar great distances over the countryside and are good at moving around between trees and shrubs. This similarity in wing shape suggests that Quetzalcoatlus hunted over forests and plains.

Quetzalcoatlus had the longest neck of any pterosaur (about 3 metres) and the longest head (about 2.5 metres).

The wing bones and muscles had to be tremendously strong to carry such a large head crest.

Strong membranes formed the wing's surface. Stiff fibres inside helped them to hold their shape and to fold away when not in use.

Most of a pterosaur's wing was supported by a gigantic fourth finger. This finger was made up of four slim, cylindrical bones.

READY FOR TAKE OFF!

Quetzalcoatlus could fold away its wings to walk and run on all fours. If danger threatened, it would quickly launch into the air. When grounded, it was similar in size to a giraffe. In fact, with its long, slender neck and slim legs, Quetzalcoatlus was a bit like a giraffe with wings!

CRYOLOPHOSAURUS

Cryolophosaurus (cry-oh-loaf-oh-saw-rus) was discovered in the frozen ground of Mount Kirkpatrick, Antarctica, just 650 kilometres away from the South Pole. This makes it the most southerly dinosaur ever found.

This new dinosaur was a mid-sized, two-legged predator with a strange crest on its head. Its name means 'frozen crested lizard'.

 ## JURASSIC ANTARCTICA

When Cryolophosaurus was alive, Antarctica was further north than it is today (above right). The world was warmer too, so there were no ice caps or freezing temperatures. Fossil trees show that Antarctica was forested then (above left)and must have been home to many different kinds of dinosaurs and other animals. The creatures that lived there would have had to cope with low (but not freezing) temperatures in winter.

CRYOLOPHOSAURUS
(cry-oh-loaf-oh-saw-rus)

WHEN	Jurassic 183-189 mya
WHERE	Antarctica
SIZE	6m long
WEIGHT	350kg
DIET	Carnivorous
SPEED	24km/h
DANGER	HIGH

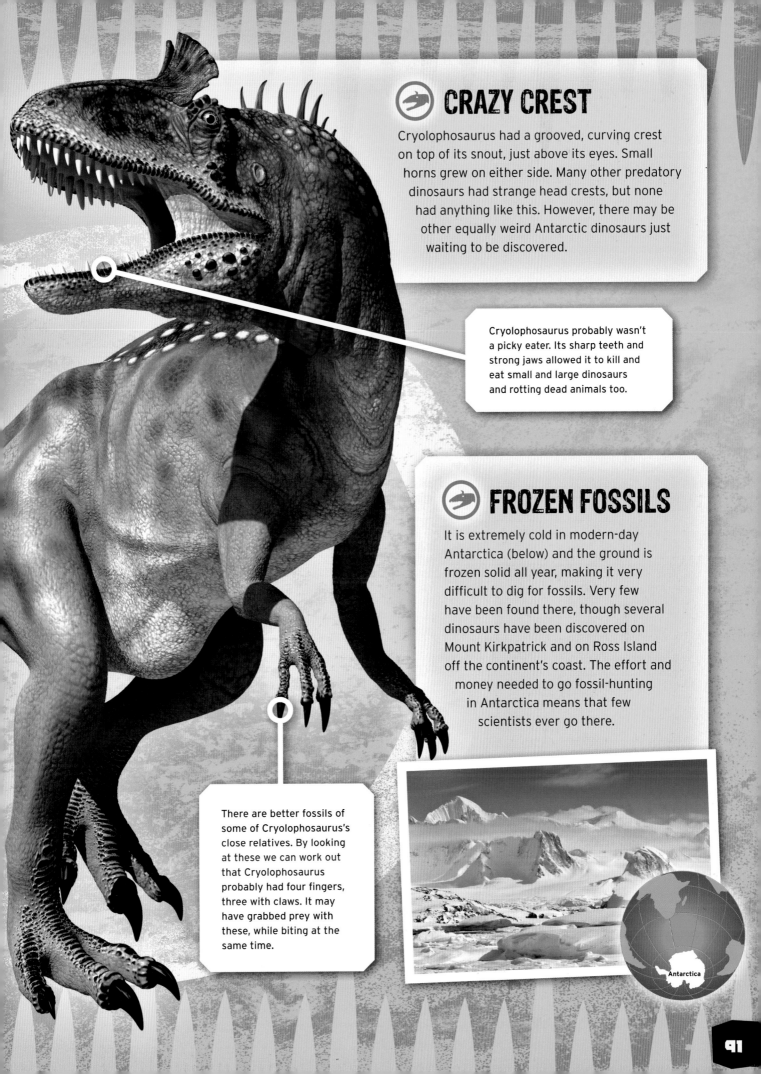

CRAZY CREST

Cryolophosaurus had a grooved, curving crest on top of its snout, just above its eyes. Small horns grew on either side. Many other predatory dinosaurs had strange head crests, but none had anything like this. However, there may be other equally weird Antarctic dinosaurs just waiting to be discovered.

Cryolophosaurus probably wasn't a picky eater. Its sharp teeth and strong jaws allowed it to kill and eat small and large dinosaurs and rotting dead animals too.

FROZEN FOSSILS

It is extremely cold in modern-day Antarctica (below) and the ground is frozen solid all year, making it very difficult to dig for fossils. Very few have been found there, though several dinosaurs have been discovered on Mount Kirkpatrick and on Ross Island off the continent's coast. The effort and money needed to go fossil-hunting in Antarctica means that few scientists ever go there.

There are better fossils of some of Cryolophosaurus's close relatives. By looking at these we can work out that Cryolophosaurus probably had four fingers, three with claws. It may have grabbed prey with these, while biting at the same time.

Antarctica

MOST PICKY EATER!

SHUVUUIA

The 'pickiest' dinosaur of them all was an insect-eater called Shuvuuia (shoo-voo-ya).

Its slender skull, tiny teeth, short muscular arms and gigantic thumb claws show that it broke into rotten wood and insect nests in search of food. This was an extremely unusual and specialised lifestyle for a dinosaur – most of which were plant-eaters or predators.

Shuvuuia had long, slender legs. It must have relied on running fast to escape from hungry predators.

 ## CLEVER CLAWS

Shuvuuia had powerful arms with block-shaped hands and gigantic curved thumb claws (see above). These arms and claws are similar to those of modern animals that break into insect nests, like armadillos and pangolins. Shuvuuia would have used its thumb claw like a miniature pickaxe, jabbing it into wood or insect nests. It would then pull back hard to break open the food store.

SHUVUUIA
(shoo-voo-ya)

WHEN	Cretaceous 74-84 mya
WHERE	Mongolia
SIZE	1m long
WEIGHT	3.5kg
DIET	Insectivorous
SPEED	48km/h
DANGER	NONE

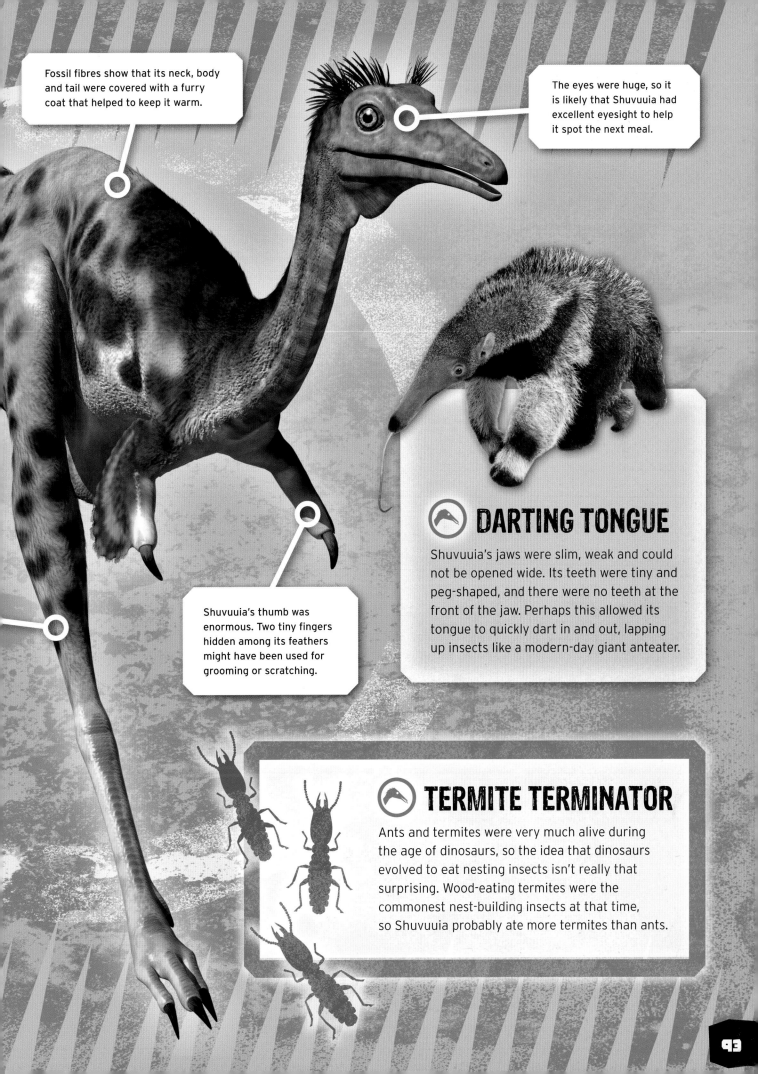

Fossil fibres show that its neck, body and tail were covered with a furry coat that helped to keep it warm.

The eyes were huge, so it is likely that Shuvuuia had excellent eyesight to help it spot the next meal.

Shuvuuia's thumb was enormous. Two tiny fingers hidden among its feathers might have been used for grooming or scratching.

DARTING TONGUE

Shuvuuia's jaws were slim, weak and could not be opened wide. Its teeth were tiny and peg-shaped, and there were no teeth at the front of the jaw. Perhaps this allowed its tongue to quickly dart in and out, lapping up insects like a modern-day giant anteater.

TERMITE TERMINATOR

Ants and termites were very much alive during the age of dinosaurs, so the idea that dinosaurs evolved to eat nesting insects isn't really that surprising. Wood-eating termites were the commonest nest-building insects at that time, so Shuvuuia probably ate more termites than ants.

MOST TEETH!

EDMONTOSAURUS

Duckbill dinosaur Edmontosaurus (ed-mon-toe-saw-rus) boasted more than 1,000 diamond-shaped teeth, which makes it the toothiest dinosaur ever.

Arranged in blocks called tooth batteries, they were used for shredding plants. Only the teeth at the very edge of each battery were used at any one time. New teeth replaced the old ones as they wore down.

🦕 TOOTHY DUCKBILL

Edmontosaurus had a broad duck-like beak to grab plants. But while ducks swallow their food whole, Edmontosaurus probably bit off mouthfuls of tough plants such as leaves, conifer branches and ferns (below), stuffing the food into its cheeks. It then shredded the material with its tooth batteries to make it easier to digest.

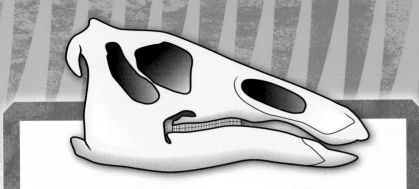

EDMONTOSAURUS
(ed-mon-toe-saw-rus)

WHEN	Cretaceous 65-61 mya
WHERE	USA, Canada
SIZE	9m long
WEIGHT	About 4 tonnes
DIET	Herbivorous
SPEED	Up to 40km/h
DANGER	LOW

GRINDING JAWS

Edmontosaurus had a special hinge in the bones of the face. This allowed it to move part of its skull from side to side and grind down leaves and twigs with its teeth. This special chewing style was unique to the hadrosaurs – the name given to the group of duckbill dinosaurs.

Big eye sockets and fossil ear bones show that Edmontosaurus had large eyes and sensitive hearing. It needed to be on the lookout for its ultimate enemy as it fed – Tyrannosaurus rex.

Edmontosaurus might also have used its beaky mouth to grab plants from shallow water.

Most prehistoric plants were difficult to digest and did not contain a lot of energy. This meant plant-eaters had to consume a large amount of vegetation every day to get enough energy to survive.

BITING BEAK

We know quite a lot about the beak of Edmontosaurus because in one fossil it did not rot away as usual. Instead the beak and skin mummified (dried out) before the dinosaur fossilized. From this we can see that the beak was made of the same horn-like material as the beaks of modern turtles and birds.

BIGGEST NEST

MACROELONGATOOLITHUS

The biggest dinosaur nest found so far was about 3 metres across and contained 28 long cylinder-shaped eggs, each about the length of a rugby ball (about 30 centimetres).

The eggs found in this nest are called Macroelongatoolithus (mack-roe-ee-long-ga-too-lith-us). They are the longest dinosaur eggs ever found – but not the largest (see p56/57).

BIG IS BEST

To get an idea of just how big this nest was, just compare it with the nests of these modern animals.

CROCODILE NEST
➡ **1** METRE ACROSS

EAGLE NEST
➡ **2** METRES ACROSS

MACROELONGATOOLITHUS NEST
➡ **3** METRES ACROSS

The eggs in the giant nest were laid in pairs. A full clutch of nearly 30 eggs would have taken many days to lay.

WHO'S THE MUM?

It's very difficult to work out which fossil nest belonged to which dinosaur. It's only possible when unhatched dinosaurs are found inside eggs, or dead fossilized parents are found on top. It's thought that the Macroelongatoolithus eggs were laid by a large dinosaur called an oviraptor – most likely the 8 metre-long oviraptor called Gigantoraptor.

MACROELONGATOOLITHUS NEST
(mack-roe-ee-long-ga-too-lith-us)

WHEN	Cretaceous 90-70 mya
WHERE	China
SIZE	3m wide
CONTAINS	28 eggs
EGG SIZE	30cm long
EGG WEIGHT	5kg each
EGG SHAPE	Cylindrical with blunt ends

 # RECORD-BREAKING NEST

How does the giant Macroelongatoolithus nest match up to other record-breaking nests? Some modern-day birds build enormous nests and add to them year after year, so the nests become vast. The biggest nest of all is that of the Australian Mallee fowl (below). These birds build huge mounds of rotting plant material. A large mound can be 4.5 metres tall and nearly 11 metres wide – that's nearly four times as wide as the Macroelongatoolithus nest!

We know that small dinosaurs sat on their nests to guard them and perhaps keep their eggs warm. Maybe the big dinosaur that laid these eggs did the same.

Experts argue over whether dinosaur eggs were covered or left exposed to the air. They might have been hidden and protected by leaves or sand.

BIGGEST ARMOURED DINOSAUR

ANKYLOSAURUS

Many of the tank-like armoured dinosaurs were big, but the largest of all was the mighty Ankylosaurus (an-ky-low-saw-rus) – an enormous, club-tailed monster that weighed as much as a large elephant.

Most of its huge neck, body and tail was covered by armour plates and it had a massive tail club. Ankylosaurus lived alongside deadly predators such as Tyrannosaurus rex (see p10/11 and p58/59), so its awesome bulk would have given it much-needed protection.

The huge horned head was more than 50 centimetres wide at the back. It could have been used in shoving matches with other ankylosaurs.

🛡 THE BIG IDEA

Being huge was definitely an advantage for this mighty living tank. Just like a modern elephant, Ankylosaurus would have been strong enough and heavy enough to push over trees if it wanted to eat leaves or fruit that were out of reach. As well as being bulky enough to force its way through undergrowth, its thick skin and armour would have protected it from spiky or prickly plants.

ANKYLOSAURUS
(an-ky-low-saw-rus)

WHEN	Cretaceous 65-70 mya
WHERE	USA
SIZE	7m long
WEIGHT	About 6 tonnes
DIET	Herbivorous
SPEED	Up to 24km/h
DANGER	MEDIUM

TOP 5 ARMOURED DINOSAURS

Here are the top 5 most heavily-plated armoured dinosaurs from the Cretaceous period.

1 ➡ **ANKYLOSAURUS** NORTH AMERICA
2 ➡ **EUOPLOCEPHALUS** NORTH AMERICA
3 ➡ **SAICHANIA** MONGOLIA
4 ➡ **TARCHIA** MONGOLIA
5 ➡ **GASTONIA** USA

The body was broad and rounded. Inside there was an enormous gut for digesting plant food. At the top of its back, the biggest Ankylosaurus would have been about 1.5 metres off the ground.

SLEDGEHAMMER TAIL

So far, only one Ankylosaurus tail club has been discovered, so it's possible that other individuals had differently-shaped clubs. The one that has been found was long and flattened from top to bottom: it was a monster-sized weapon for a monster-sized dinosaur!

The club tail was about 60 centimetres long and 30 centimetres wide – that's about the size of a large wastepaper bin.

MASSIVE MUSCLES

Ankylosaurus had thigh muscles about six times wider than an adult human's. The base of its tail was muscly too. These super-sized muscles would have given Ankylosaurus enormous strength in its tail and back legs for swishing its tail club at predators.

FANCIEST FEATHERS

MICRORAPTOR

Early prehistoric birds such as Archaeopteryx (see p72/73) had feathers, but surprisingly many other types of dinosaur did too.

The fanciest feathers of all belonged to a tiny dinosaur called Microraptor (my-crow-rap-tor). It had a crested head, fan-shaped feathers at the end of its tail and enormously-long arm and hand feathers. Most surprising of all, the feathers on its legs were almost as long as those on its arms.

The tail was covered with small feathers, but those at the end were longer and spread outwards to form a fan shape.

TWIN WING

The long leg and foot feathers of Microraptor are unique and nothing like them exists today. Some experts think that the leg feathers were used in some kind of flapping or gliding flight. Perhaps Microraptor might have been a sort of 'biplane' dinosaur, holding its arm and leg feathers in parallel.

Curved claws were found on the second toes of the feet. They were probably used for killing prey.

MICRORAPTOR
(my-crow-rap-tor)

WHEN	Cretaceous 125-120 mya
WHERE	China
SIZE	70cm long
WEIGHT	600g
DIET	Carnivorous
SPEED	40km/h
DANGER	NONE

FANTASTIC FEATHERS

Here's a list of the top five fanciest-feathered mini-dinosaurs.

1 ➡ MICRORAPTOR
LONG ARM AND LEG FEATHERS, TAIL FAN AND FEATHERY CREST

2 ➡ EPIDEXIPTERYX
GIANT TAIL FEATHERS

3 ➡ ANCHIORNIS
A BUSHY HEAD CREST AND BIG ARM AND LEG FEATHERS

4 ➡ SINORNITHOSAURUS
A LARGE VERSION OF MICRORAPTOR, BUT WITH SHORTER FEATHERS

5 ➡ CAUDIPTERYX
LONG HAND FEATHERS AND A V-SHAPED TAIL FAN

We don't know what colour Microraptor's feathers were, but they may have been colourful like some modern birds.

FEATHERY FINGERS

It is almost impossible to tell the difference between early birds and bird-like dinosaurs such as Microraptor. The arm and hand feathers of Microraptor were incredibly long and provided it with long, slender wings. The feathers grew off the fingers as well as the arm bones, exactly as they do in modern birds.

The long thin legs look suited for fast running, but those big feathers might have got in Microraptor's way!

SMALLEST BRAIN!

STEGOSAURUS

Most plant-eating dinosaurs had very small brains, but the brain of the giant-plated dinosaur Stegosaurus (steg-oh-saw-rus) was particularly tiny.

The brain of an adult human is about 25 times bigger! Very little of Stegosaurus's brain was actually used for thinking. Most of it was devoted to smell and other senses. In fact, the part used for thinking was about the size of a walnut.

⊙ SIMPLE STEGOSAURUS

The small brain suggests that Stegosaurus was mostly driven by instinct and that it didn't do much complicated thinking. But this is true of virtually all animals, so it's not as if Stegosaurus was at all unusual! Despite its tiny brain, Stegosaurus was not especially stupid. Most of the world's animals (like insects and fish) get by just fine with their small brains.

The part of the brain dealing with smell was quite large, so Stegosaurus must have been good at sniffing out tasty plants to eat.

⊙ TWO BRAINS?

An early idea about Stegosaurus was that a space in its spine housed a second brain, which was used to control the back half of its body. In fact, spaces like this are common in both large dinosaurs and modern birds and they don't house a brain. Instead, an organ called the glycogen body goes there.

Stegosaurus would have relied on powerful sweeps of its huge tail to defend itself against predators, rather than brain power!

The glycogen body in the spine might have been an energy store, or it may have helped the animal control its balance.

⊙ SMALLEST BRAINS

Here are the top 5 dinosaurs with particularly small brains for their size.

1 ➡ STEGOSAURUS
2 ➡ DIPLODOCUS
3 ➡ KENTROSAURUS
4 ➡ EUOPLOCEPHALUS
5 ➡ TRICERATOPS

⊙ BRAIN POWER

Predators tend to have bigger brains, as they need more brain power to hunt prey. Simple plant-eaters like Stegosaurus (right) didn't need as much brain power as cunning, fast-moving predators and so tended to have smaller brains for their body size.

MOST DINOSAUR FOSSILS FOUND

PSITTACOSAURUS

The small, parrot-beaked dinosaur Psittacosaurus (sitt-ack-uh-saw-rus) is known from many hundreds of skeletons, possibly thousands, including tiny babies, half-grown youngsters and adults.

These fossils provide lots of information on how this dinosaur lived and what it looked like. In fact, we can say with confidence that we know more about Psittacosaurus than any other dinosaur.

Some Psittacosaurus fossils are so well preserved that they have patches of skin on them. One unusual Psittacosaurus fossil even has a strange fuzzy patch on its tail (see p76/77).

Many Psittacosaurus fossils have masses of small stones in the stomach. Maybe Psittacosaurus used these to help mash up its tough plant food.

 SUCCESS STORY

All sorts of different sized and shaped Psittacosaurus fossils have been found. Some had huge cheek horns and others had large horns on their noses. They've been discovered across a huge area and from rocks 20 million years apart. This all means that there were lots of different species of Psittacosaurus, some as different from each other as lions are from tigers.

PSITTACOSAURUS

(sitt-ack-uh-saw-rus)

WHEN	Cretaceous 105-115 mya
WHERE	Mongolia
SIZE	1m long
WEIGHT	About 6kg
DIET	Herbivorous
SPEED	Up to 40km/h
DANGER	LOW

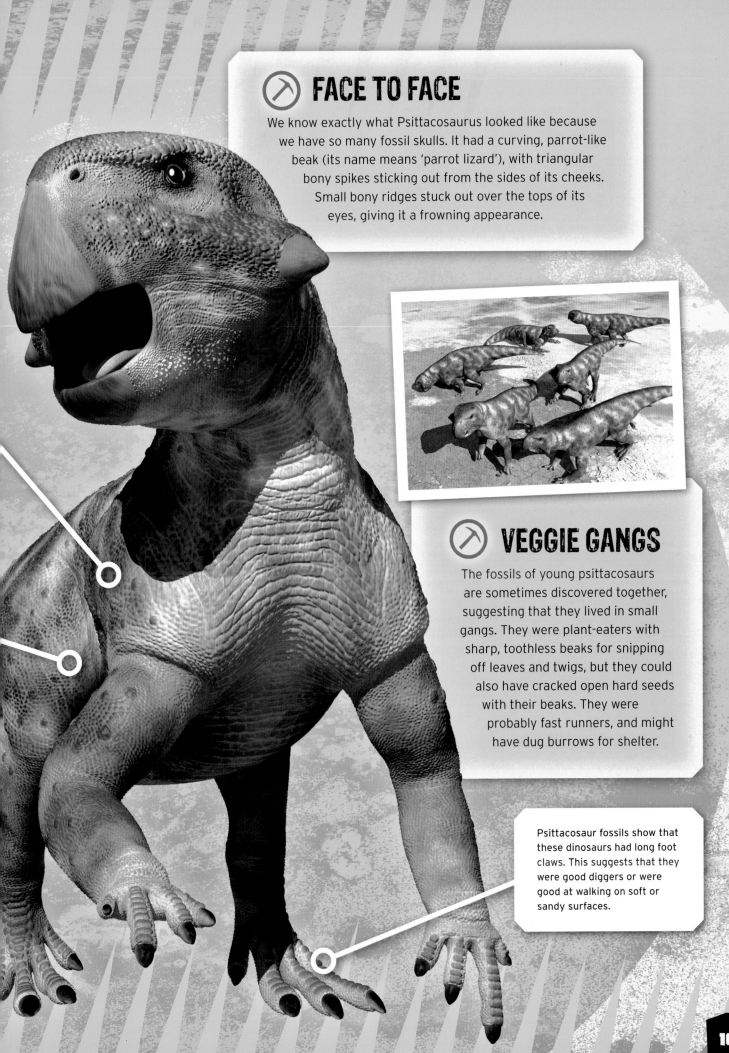

⚒ FACE TO FACE

We know exactly what Psittacosaurus looked like because we have so many fossil skulls. It had a curving, parrot-like beak (its name means 'parrot lizard'), with triangular bony spikes sticking out from the sides of its cheeks. Small bony ridges stuck out over the tops of its eyes, giving it a frowning appearance.

⚒ VEGGIE GANGS

The fossils of young psittacosaurs are sometimes discovered together, suggesting that they lived in small gangs. They were plant-eaters with sharp, toothless beaks for snipping off leaves and twigs, but they could also have cracked open hard seeds with their beaks. They were probably fast runners, and might have dug burrows for shelter.

Psittacosaur fossils show that these dinosaurs had long foot claws. This suggests that they were good diggers or were good at walking on soft or sandy surfaces.

BIGGEST SEA REPTILE

SHONISAURUS

Shonisaurus (shon-ee-saw-rus) – a fish-shaped ichthyosaur from North America – grew to at least 21 metres in length, making it the biggest ocean reptile ever.

It was one of several ancient marine reptiles that reached an enormous size. Like the biggest modern whales, it was not a powerful predator, but probably preyed on small animals, such as squid.

 SEA GIANTS

Because water supports their weight, animals that live in water can reach much greater sizes than land animals. Most Shonisaurus seem to have reached about 21 metres in length, but a few bones found on their own suggest that some specimens were even bigger and probably similar in size to an average-sized blue whale (up to 26 metres long).

Nobody knows what colour ichthyosaurs were. Like whales today, Shonisaurus might have been a greyish or bluish colour, to help camouflage it from prey.

The long, slender fins were up to 3 metres long and were made up of many small, disc-shaped finger bones.

SHONISAURUS
(shon-ee-saw-rus)

WHEN	Triassic 216-203 mya
WHERE	USA, Canada,
SIZE	21m long
WEIGHT	20 tonnes
DIET	Fish, squid
SPEED	7km/h
DANGER	MEDIUM

MINI MEALS?

The enormous size of Shonisaurus has led some experts to wonder whether it might have fed on tiny organisms called plankton, like some huge modern whales – though no fossil evidence has been found so far to support this idea. Whales swallow large quantities of water and plankton together. The water is pushed out of the mouth through hair-like structure in the upper jaw called baleen, trapping the plankton.

All ichthyosaurs had enormous eyes to help with hunting in deep water. We don't know for sure how big the eyes of Shonisaurus were, but they were probably about as big as a melon (20cm wide).

SUPERSIZE SEA MONSTERS

1 → **BLUE WHALE** BIGGEST MARINE MAMMAL → 33 METRES

2 → **SHONISAURUS** BIGGEST MARINE REPTILE → 21 METRES

3 → **MEGATOOTH SHARK** BIGGEST FISH EVER → 20 METRES

4 → **WHALE SHARK** BIGGEST MODERN FISH → 13 METRES

Shonisaurus

Megatooth

Diver

Blue whale

Whale shark

LONGEST JAWS!

SPINOSAURUS

Unlike most other big predatory dinosaurs, the enormous Spinosaurus (spine-oh-saw-rus) had long, narrow, crocodile-like jaws — the longest of any known dinosaur, in fact.

It probably used them to catch fish by reaching into rivers and lakes. Experts have worked out that the biggest Spinosaurus skull and lower jaw ever found was probably more than 1.7 metres long when complete. That's about the length of a bathtub.

The teeth were rounded, big and pointed — a good shape for stabbing fish.

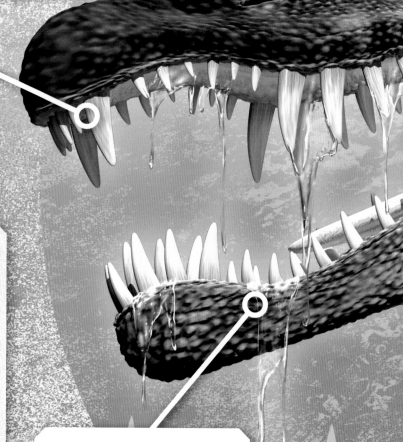

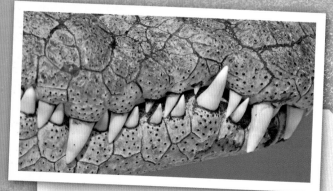

 CROCODILE SMILE

In many predatory dinosaurs, the edges of the upper and lower jaws are more or less straight. The jaws of Spinosaurus were wavy, and fitted together like a modern-day crocodile's jaws. Some of the front teeth stuck forwards as well as downwards.

The curving edges of the jaws could have helped Spinosaurus to grab fish and trap them in its mouth.

SPINOSAURUS
(spine-oh-saw-rus)

WHEN	Cretaceous 95-112 mya
WHERE	North Africa
SIZE	18m long
WEIGHT	10 tonnes
DIET	Carnivorous
SPEED	32km/h
DANGER	HIGH

WATERPROOF

Spinosaurus had nostrils that were further up and closer to the eyes than other dinosaurs. Perhaps this was to help Spinosaurus to breathe when the tip of its snout was in the water grabbing fish.

LOOK AT ME!

Spinosaurus had a bony crest sticking up from the top of its snout, just in front of its eyes. This seems to be fragile and probably wasn't used in fighting. It may have been brightly-coloured for impressing mates.

BIGGEST GRAVE

COELOPHYSIS

Fossil animals are usually found on their own, but sometimes lots of the same kind of animal are found together.

These big fossil graves are called death assemblages and they happen when lots of animals are killed at the same time. The biggest dinosaur death assemblage ever found consisted of hundreds of skeletons of the small, early meat-eater Coelophysis (see-low-fye-sis). It was discovered at Ghost Ranch, New Mexico, USA, in 1947.

The discovery of so many Coelophysis together might show that they lived in packs or family groups.

THE VICTIMS

The Ghost Ranch skeletons showed that Coelophysis was a slim predator with a long, narrow snout and a notch on the tip of the upper jaw. Its slender jaws and teeth suggest that it caught small reptiles, fish and other animals, but it was also big enough to attack animals its own size.

THE LAST MEAL

Some of the Coelophysis skeletons at Ghost Ranch contained the bones of smaller reptiles inside their stomachs – so for a while it was thought Coelophysis were cannibals who ate smaller members of their own kind. However, we now know that the reptiles in their stomachs were an early relative of crocodiles.

MYSTERY DEATH

Nobody knows for sure why so many dinosaurs gathered in the same place before they died. Perhaps they were attracted by a rich source of food, such as a shoal of spawning fish, and were killed by poisonous gases released from a volcano.

TOP 5 EXPLANATIONS FOR MYSTERY DEATHS

1 → POISONING
BY TOXIC GASES RELEASED FROM VOLCANOES OR LAKES

2 → SUFFOCATION
BY VOLCANIC ASH

3 → DROWNING
WHILE TRYING TO CROSS A FLOODED RIVER

4 → SUFFOCATION
BY RAGING SAND STORMS

5 → STARVATION
AFTER GETTING STUCK IN MUD

Fossil hunters have yet to find evidence for the skin covering of Coelophysis. It might have been scaly, or covered in short, hair-like feathers.

Some of the Ghost Ranch fossils are bigger, with thicker bones than the others. No-one is sure if these were the males or the females.

COELOPHYSIS
(see-low-fye-sis)

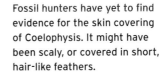

WHEN	Triassic 203-216 mya
WHERE	USA
SIZE	3m long
WEIGHT	25kg
DIET	Carnivorous
SPEED	48km/h
DANGER	MEDIUM

BIGGEST DUCKBILL!

ZHUCHENGOSAURUS

The sauropods weren't the only giants of the prehistoric world. Some duckbill dinosaurs were supersized too. The biggest was Zhuchengosaurus (zoo-chen-go-saw-rus) from China.

At almost 17 metres long and as heavy as three male African elephants, it was one of the largest land animals of all time.

 BIG QUESTION

Duckbill dinosaurs gradually evolved to become huge, and several grew to giant, sauropod-like proportions. But was there an advantage to growing so big? Maybe, like modern elephants, they used their size to help scare off big predators, or to reach tall plants.

A duckbill this big would have made giant, three-toed footprints about 1 metre long. Tracks like this have been discovered in North America, but not in China where Zhuchengosaurus was found.

Like all duckbills, it would have had four fingers, three of which were used for walking on. The hand and arm bones must have been very strong to bear its great weight.

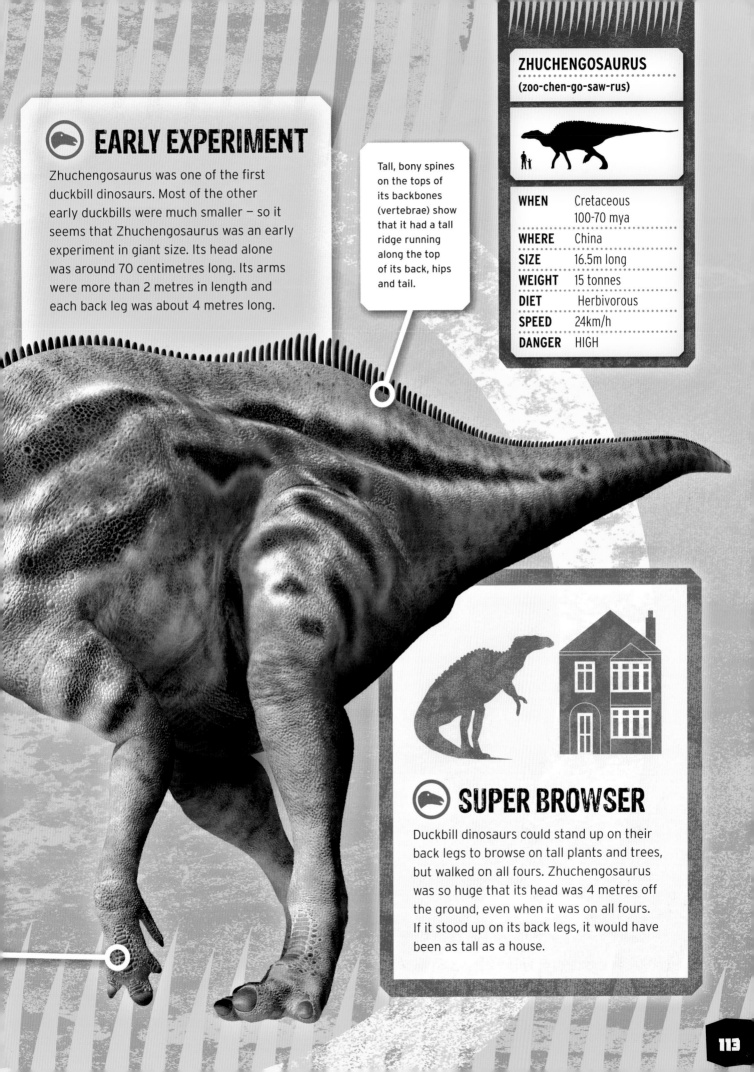

⬤ EARLY EXPERIMENT

Zhuchengosaurus was one of the first duckbill dinosaurs. Most of the other early duckbills were much smaller – so it seems that Zhuchengosaurus was an early experiment in giant size. Its head alone was around 70 centimetres long. Its arms were more than 2 metres in length and each back leg was about 4 metres long.

Tall, bony spines on the tops of its backbones (vertebrae) show that it had a tall ridge running along the top of its back, hips and tail.

ZHUCHENGOSAURUS
(zoo-chen-go-saw-rus)

WHEN	Cretaceous 100-70 mya
WHERE	China
SIZE	16.5m long
WEIGHT	15 tonnes
DIET	Herbivorous
SPEED	24km/h
DANGER	HIGH

⬤ SUPER BROWSER

Duckbill dinosaurs could stand up on their back legs to browse on tall plants and trees, but walked on all fours. Zhuchengosaurus was so huge that its head was 4 metres off the ground, even when it was on all fours. If it stood up on its back legs, it would have been as tall as a house.

CRAZIEST CREST!

PARASAUROLOPHUS

Several duckbill dinosaurs had huge bony crests on their heads, but Parasaurolophus (par-ah-saw-ra-low-fuss) had the craziest.

At one metre long, it was the biggest crest of any dinosaur and was filled with strange looping passages which may have helped it to make loud, deep, honking noises. For this reason, Parasaurolophus is nicknamed the 'trombone duckbill'.

A web of skin might have connected the crest to the rest of the neck. We know from mummified specimens that at least some duckbills had skin webs like this.

Parasaurolophus may also have used its impressive crest to show off to other dinosaurs and attract a mate.

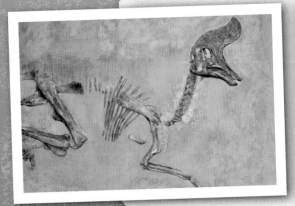

WHO'S WHO?

Parasaurolophus had a long, fairly straight crest, but this is not true for all kinds of duckbill dinosaurs. Some had plate-shaped crests. Others, like Lambeosaurus (left), had axe or fan-shaped crests. Perhaps they recognised their own kind by looking at their crests.

TOP 5 CRAZY CRESTS

1 → PARASAUROLOPHUS   2 → OLOROTITAN   3 → TSINTAOSAURUS   4 → CHARONOSAURUS   5 → LAMBEOSAURUS

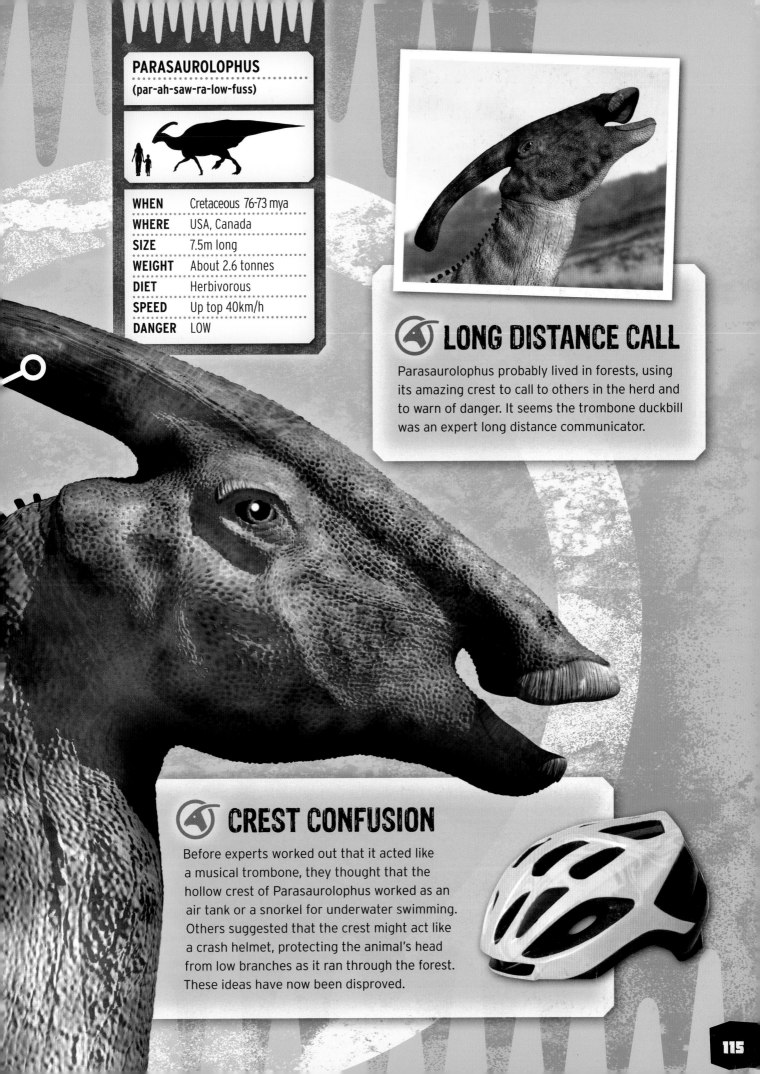

PARASAUROLOPHUS
(par-ah-saw-ra-low-fuss)

WHEN	Cretaceous 76-73 mya
WHERE	USA, Canada
SIZE	7.5m long
WEIGHT	About 2.6 tonnes
DIET	Herbivorous
SPEED	Up top 40km/h
DANGER	LOW

LONG DISTANCE CALL

Parasaurolophus probably lived in forests, using its amazing crest to call to others in the herd and to warn of danger. It seems the trombone duckbill was an expert long distance communicator.

CREST CONFUSION

Before experts worked out that it acted like a musical trombone, they thought that the hollow crest of Parasaurolophus worked as an air tank or a snorkel for underwater swimming. Others suggested that the crest might act like a crash helmet, protecting the animal's head from low branches as it ran through the forest. These ideas have now been disproved.

SPIKIEST DINOSAUR!

EDMONTONIA

A plant-eating dinosaur from the North of America called Edmontonia (ed-mon-toe-nee-ah) wins the prize for being the spikiest dinosaur of all time.

Blunt spikes stuck out sideways from its body, but the long, sharply-pointed spines on its shoulders and neck were most amazing of all. They look like the ideal weapons for fending off predators such as Tyrannosaurus rex.

Two of the largest spikes were forked near the bottom. This might have been so that two Edmontonia could lock their spines together to fight for mates or territory.

 SUPER SPIKES

The longest spikes grew from the shoulders. When the dinosaur was alive, these spikes would have been even longer and sharper than they appear in fossils, because they had a horny material covering them.

Large armour plates covered the surfaces and sides of Edmontonia's skull. Bony lumps around its eyes and cheeks gave extra protection.

SQUAT AND SPIKY

Like most armoured dinosaurs, Edmontonia had a very wide and shallow body. Its back was almost flat, its four legs were quite short and muscular and it had a long tail. All these features made Edmontonia very stable and kept its weight close to the ground. It would have been difficult for predators such as Tyrannosaurus rex to push it over in a fight!

WHEN	Cretaceous 65-70 mya
WHERE	USA, Canada
SIZE	6m long
WEIGHT	About 3 tonnes
DIET	Herbivorous
SPEED	24km/h
DANGER	MEDIUM

The sharp edges of the spikes would have been great for injuring enemies and rivals.

 # CHARGE!

Edmontonia's longest spikes were angled forwards, so they would only be useful if the animal turned to face an attacker. Running away or squatting on the ground would leave the animal's unprotected hips and tail vulnerable to attack. Like modern-day bulls and rhinos, Edmontonia could well have charged when faced by a predator.

The body was protected by bands of bony armour. Massive, square armour plates were arranged in rows across the top of the neck and helped to protect the neck during fighting.

WEIRDEST LOOKING!

THERIZINOSAURUS

Therizinosaurus (thair-ee-zine-uh-saw-rus), found in Mongolia, was one of the weirdest-looking dinosaurs of them all.

With its feathers, long claws and big belly, it looked like a cross between a camel and a massive shaggy goose with teeth! It probably walked with an upright posture – unlike most other dinosaurs.

Therizinosaurus is so weird that experts argued for decades about what sort of dinosaur it was.

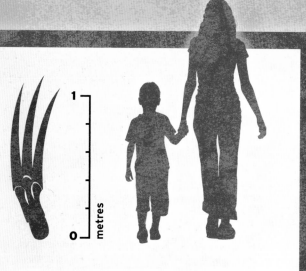

 **CRAZY CLAWS**

Therizinosaurus had wide, short, four-toed feet with long, curved foot claws. Its hind legs were short and its body was very wide, so it would probably have been a poor runner. This might explain why it had incredibly long hand claws (1 metre long). Unable to run away from predators, it probably fought them off, or simply scared them away.

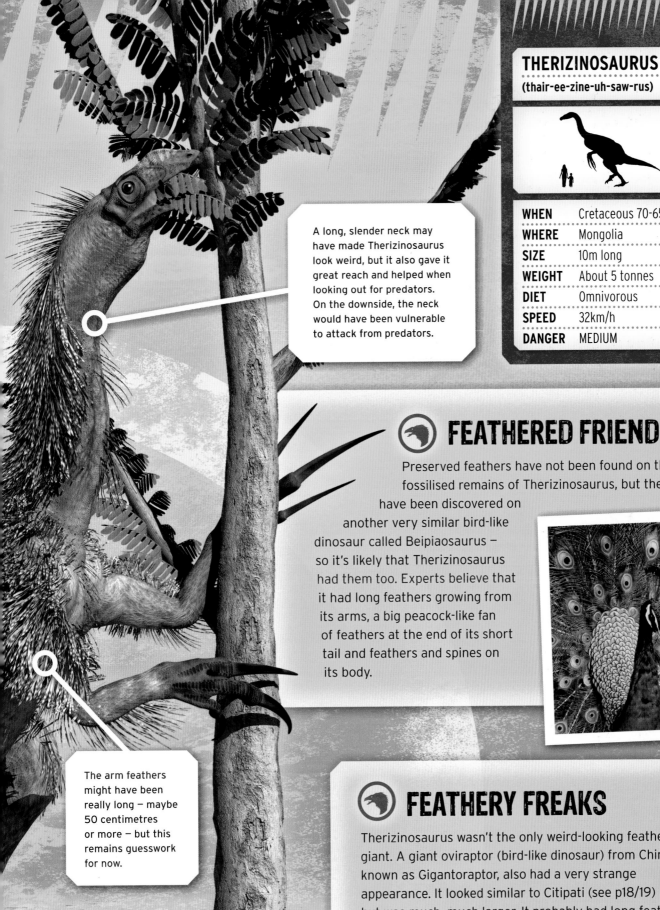

WHEN	Cretaceous 70-65 mya
WHERE	Mongolia
SIZE	10m long
WEIGHT	About 5 tonnes
DIET	Omnivorous
SPEED	32km/h
DANGER	MEDIUM

A long, slender neck may have made Therizinosaurus look weird, but it also gave it great reach and helped when looking out for predators. On the downside, the neck would have been vulnerable to attack from predators.

🦅 FEATHERED FRIEND

Preserved feathers have not been found on the fossilised remains of Therizinosaurus, but they have been discovered on another very similar bird-like dinosaur called Beipiaosaurus – so it's likely that Therizinosaurus had them too. Experts believe that it had long feathers growing from its arms, a big peacock-like fan of feathers at the end of its short tail and feathers and spines on its body.

The arm feathers might have been really long – maybe 50 centimetres or more – but this remains guesswork for now.

🦅 FEATHERY FREAKS

Therizinosaurus wasn't the only weird-looking feathery giant. A giant oviraptor (bird-like dinosaur) from China, known as Gigantoraptor, also had a very strange appearance. It looked similar to Citipati (see p18/19) but was much, much larger. It probably had long feathers on its arms, a fan of feathers on its tail and shaggy feathers covering its body. It might even have built the biggest dinosaur nest ever found (see p96/97).

ULTIMATE KILLING MACHINE

UTAHRAPTOR

Enormous, bird-like Utahraptor (yoo-tah-rap-tor) was one of the most well-armed predators.

It was a ferocious dinosaur with a jawful of terrifying teeth and giant curved claws on its feet and hands. These fearsome weapons made it the ultimate killing machine.

 SLASH AND GRAB

Unlike humans, Utahraptor could not turn its wrists to make its hands face the ground. Instead, the hands were fixed in a clapping position. They would have been used for grabbing small animals, such as mammals or baby dinosaurs, or for slashing the skin of large dinosaurs.

Utahraptor was similar in weight to a large modern-day brown bear.

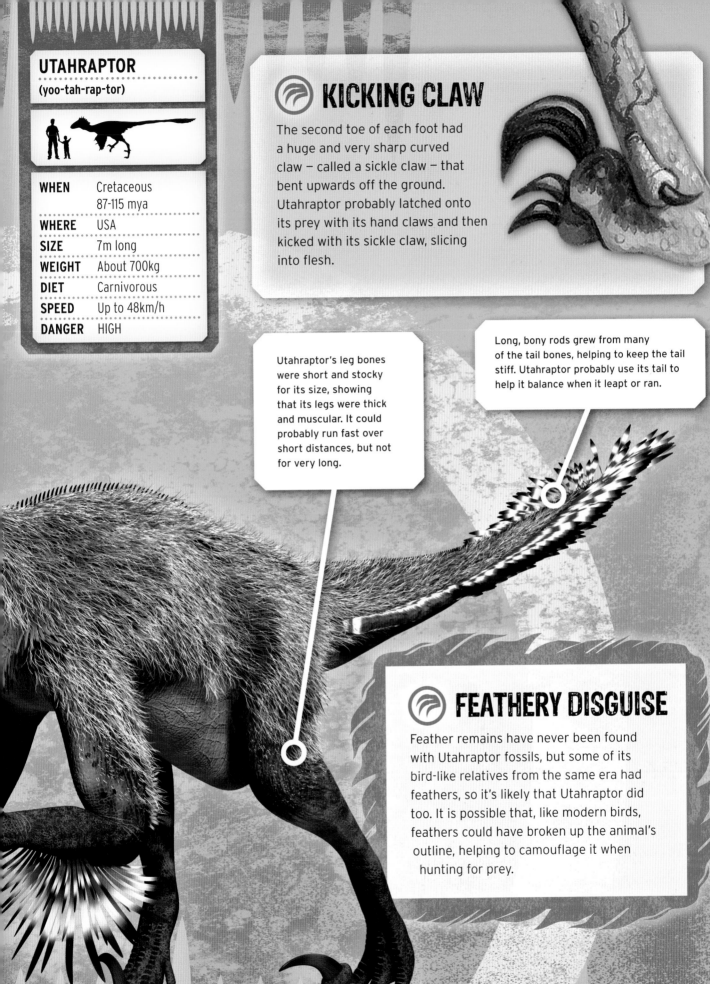

UTAHRAPTOR

(yoo-tah-rap-tor)

WHEN	Cretaceous 87-115 mya
WHERE	USA
SIZE	7m long
WEIGHT	About 700kg
DIET	Carnivorous
SPEED	Up to 48km/h
DANGER	HIGH

KICKING CLAW

The second toe of each foot had a huge and very sharp curved claw – called a sickle claw – that bent upwards off the ground. Utahraptor probably latched onto its prey with its hand claws and then kicked with its sickle claw, slicing into flesh.

Utahraptor's leg bones were short and stocky for its size, showing that its legs were thick and muscular. It could probably run fast over short distances, but not for very long.

Long, bony rods grew from many of the tail bones, helping to keep the tail stiff. Utahraptor probably use its tail to help it balance when it leapt or ran.

FEATHERY DISGUISE

Feather remains have never been found with Utahraptor fossils, but some of its bird-like relatives from the same era had feathers, so it's likely that Utahraptor did too. It is possible that, like modern birds, feathers could have broken up the animal's outline, helping to camouflage it when hunting for prey.

MOST COLOURFUL

ANCHIORNIS

Anchiornis (an-kee-orr-nis), a small feathered dinosaur from China, is the most colourful dinosaur that we know of.

It had a reddish head crest, a mottled red and grey face, and striking patterns of black and white on its feathered wings and legs. Other non-feathered dinosaurs may have been more colourful, but we don't yet know for sure.

 COLOUR SECRETS

Experts can now work out the colours of feathered dinosaurs by studying the material in fossilised feathers that creates colour. Many feathered fossils have dark bands preserved across their surface, which represent the original pattern. Tiny cells called melanosomes, which help produce colours, are sometimes preserved too. It it not yet possible to find out this information for non-feathered dinosaurs.

STRIKING CONTRAST

Anchiornis's body was mostly grey. The long feathers on its arms and hands were mostly white, but they had black tips and rows of black spots. Long leg feathers were also white and spotted with black. When Anchiornis spread its feathers and raised its crest, the result would have been striking, rather like a modern-day hoopoe.

⊛ NO BIRD

Anchiornis looked rather like a pigeon-sized bird. It had long arm, leg and tail feathers, a bushy crest and a covering of short body feathers. However, it also had features that birds don't have, such as a short blunt snout. In fact, it was actually a type of dinosaur called a troodontid and was related to the much larger Troodon (right).

The reddish crest — similar to that of many modern birds — may have been used in display, to impress mates.

The long arm and hand feathers would have mostly hidden the arm from view. Only the finger claws would have been visible.

Surprisingly, Anchiornis had feathers all the way down to the tips of its toes. Modern birds with feathery toes tend to live in cold places.

ANCHIORNIS
(an-kee-orr-nis)

WHEN	Jurassic 165-155 mya
WHERE	China
SIZE	40cm long
WEIGHT	250g
DIET	Carnivorous
SPEED	Up to 40km/h
DANGER	NONE

MOST NORTHERLY DINOSAUR

TROODON

Fossils of big-brained, big-eyed Troodon (troo-uh-don) have been discovered in the rocks of northern Alaska in the far north of the world, inside the Arctic Circle. Troodon would have lived for months at a time in cold winter darkness. Its combination of unusual features allowed it to become the most northerly dinosaur we know about.

Sharp, serrated teeth could have been used to chop up small animals as well as leaves and fruit.

◯ SUPER SENSES

Troodon's excellent sensory abilities and relatively big brain all helped it to survive in the cold and dark of the far north. Enormous eyes (see p30/31) let in enough light to allow it to hunt in the dark. An excellent sense of hearing helped it to pinpoint sounds made by hidden prey.

WILL EAT ANYTHING

If Troodon really did stay in the far north throughout the dark winter, it would make sense if its diet was varied. It might have eaten animals large and small, dead or alive and also plant material such as leaves or fruit. Studies of Troodon's curved, serrated teeth indicate that they were used to kill and slice up animal prey, but could also shred leaves.

TROODON
(troo-uh-don)

WHEN	Cretaceous 70-65 mya
WHERE	USA, Canada
SIZE	2.5m long
WEIGHT	35kg
DIET	Omnivorous
SPEED	Up to 48km/h
DANGER	MEDIUM

Fossils of related species show that this type of dinosaur slept by curling its tail round its body, and tucking its head against its side for protection from the cold.

With much of its body covered by feathers, Troodon was well-insulated from the cold.

COSY COVERING

Troodon probably had feathers on its arms, legs and tail, and thick fur-like feathers on its body, like modern-day Arctic birds such as the snowy owl (right). These feathers would have helped Troodon to survive in the cold. It was probably warm-blooded, like modern-day animals that live in cold places.

BIGGEST MASS EXTINCTION!

Sixty-five million years ago, at the end of the Cretaceous period, one of the most devastating mass extinctions of all time took place. It wiped out up to eighty percent of all living things and ended the dinosaurs' reign on Earth.

One theory is that the extinction was caused by the effects of a massive asteroid (space rock) hitting Earth, but there is evidence that many groups of living things were not doing well, even before the asteroid hit.

During the Cretaceous period, shallow seas across the world dried up, destroying coastal areas and changing the climate and vegetation. These changes would have made life more difficult for the dinosaurs.

MEGA EXPLOSION

A gigantic crater in Mexico, made about 65 millions years ago, fits the asteroid theory. The Chixculub crater is more than 180 kilometres wide and was created after a rock 10 kilometres wide slammed into Earth. It hit with a force 2 million times more powerful than the biggest explosion created by humans.

Towards the end of the Cretaceous period, up to two million cubic kilometres of lava poured out of volcanic cracks in India. This filled the atmosphere with toxic gases and perhaps changed the world's climate. This may also have contributed to the extinction event.

ASTEROID IMPACT!

➡ ANIMALS AND PLANTS IN THE IMMEDIATE AREA OF THE BLAST ARE VAPORISED

➡ ANIMALS AND PLANTS WITHIN 1 KILOMETRE OF THE IMPACT ARE BURNED

➡ HEAT FROM THE BLAST CAUSES MASSIVE FIRES

➡ SHOCK WAVES CAUSE GIGANTIC TIDAL WAVES

➡ DUST THROWN INTO THE AIR BLOCKS OUT THE SUN FOR MONTHS, YEARS OR EVEN DECADES.

➡ CHEMICALS BLASTED INTO THE ATMOSPHERE CAUSE ACID RAIN

The huge asteroid would have created a brightly glowing plume extending many kilometres up into the sky and would have vaporised on impact.

Sea creatures, marine and flying reptiles, and many groups of lizards and mammals were wiped out by the extinction event. The dinosaurs were badly affected too, but they did not all die off. One branch of the dinosaur family survived – the birds.

GLOSSARY

Brow horns
Some dinosaurs such as Triceratops and Coahuilaceratops had brow horns over their eyes. Some horned dinosaurs had long brow horns, others had short ones.

Camouflage
Some living things are coloured or patterned in order to blend in with their surroundings and to hide from predators or prey. This is known as camouflage.

Campanian
A section of the Cretaceous period, from 83 to 70 million years ago. This time period was the 'golden age of the dinosaurs'. It was followed by the Maastrichtian, the last stage of the Cretaceous period.

Carnivorous
The name given to creatures that kill and eat other animals in order to gain energy and do not regularly eat plants. Sharks, tigers and Tyrannosaurus rex are examples of carnivorous animals.

Chixculub crater
A giant crater in Mexico, 180km wide, created when a giant rock from space hit the Earth at the very end of the Cretaceous period. Despite its size it is not obvious, and it was only discovered during the 1970s.

Cold-blooded
The name given to animals that rely on heat sources like the sun to keep their bodies warm. The majority of living things are cold-blooded.

Crest
Any raised ridge of bone, feathers, fur or skin on an animal's head or body can be called a crest.

Cretaceous
The section of time (known as a period) between the Jurassic and Paleocene periods. It extended from 145 to 65 million years ago. Dinosaurs dominated life on land during the Cretaceous period.

Crurotarsans
The group of reptiles that includes modern crocodilians and their fossil relatives. Many different kinds of crurotarsans existed during the Triassic period, but only crocodilians survived beyond it.

Death assemblage
A collection of once-living things, preserved close together having been killed at the same time by the same event. Death assemblages can occur as a result of floods, volcanic eruptions, droughts or famines.

Dinosaur renaissance
A renaissance is a new surge of interest in an old subject, often inspired by the creative work of one or a few people. A dinosaur renaissance occurred during the 1960s when Robert Bakker argued that dinosaurs were warm-blooded. This made experts think again at what they thought they knew about dinosaurs.

Duckbill
The popular name for the hadrosaurs – a group of plant-eating Cretaceous dinosaurs with duck-like bills and huge bulky bodies.

Extinct
A living thing is extinct if it no longer exists. If an animal is described as extinct, it means that the last surviving one of the species has died.

Evolution
The tendency of all living things to change over time. Evolution usually happens over thousands of years, but we can also watch modern plants and animals evolve over short spans of time too.

Frill
The name given to the bony shelf that sticks out backwards and upwards from the skulls of horned dinosaurs like Triceratops. Frills were small in the earliest horned dinosaurs, but became enormous in later species.

Glycogen body
A rounded organ found between the two halves of the hips in many dinosaurs and modern birds. It may have acted as an energy store or even as an organ to help control balance.

Hadrosaurs
The group of beaked, plant-eating Cretaceous dinosaurs, also known as duckbills. Many had hollow bony head crests. Examples include Parasaurolophus and Edmontosaurus.

Herbivorous
The name given to creatures that eat plants in order to gain energy and do not regularly eat animals. Herbivorous animals – called herbivores – tend to have large guts and a mouth suited to cropping plant material.

Heterodontosaurs
A group of small, probably omnivorous dinosaurs, famous for their large fangs. They also had long, clawed hands and long, slender back legs. They were one of the first groups of ornithischian dinosaurs to evolve.

Ichthyosaurs
A group of swimming, marine reptiles from the Mesozoic period. Early kinds were shaped like lizards with flippers, but most of the best known ones were fish-shaped, with dorsal fins and shark-like tails.

Jurassic
The section of time (known as a period) between the Triassic and Cretaceous periods. It extended from 199 to 145 million years ago. Dinosaurs dominated life on land during the Jurassic.

Marine
A general term used for the area covered by seas and oceans, but also used to describe the plants and animals that inhabit this area. Sharks and whales are mostly marine creatures, and so were ichthyosaurs and plesiosaurs.

Mass extinction
An event in history when a large percentage of the animal and plant species alive at the time become extinct. Mass extinctions are caused by catastrophic events, such as a massive change in climate or the impact of a giant asteroid.

Mesozoic
The huge span of time (known as an era) that extended from 250 to 65 million years ago and included the Triassic, Jurassic and Cretaceous periods. The Mesozoic Era is often known as the 'age of reptiles': it is the time when dinosaurs ruled life on land.

Omnivorous
The name given to creatures that eat both animal and plant material in order to gain energy. Humans are omnivorous, and so are pigs and bears. The bodies of omnivorous animals combine plant-eating features and meat-eating features.

Ornithischians
The group of mostly herbivorous dinosaurs that possess a special bone in the lower jaw and back-turned hip bones. Stegosaurs, ankylosaurs and hadrosaurs are all ornithischians.

Palaeontologist
A scientist devoted to palaeontology – the study of ancient life. Palaeontologists tend to specialise in a particular part of palaeontology, such as fossil plants, dinosaurs or fossil marine reptiles.

Plankton
The name given to tiny aquatic organisms that float freely in open water, both in marine habitats and in freshwater. There are different kinds of plankton, including animals, plants, microscopic bacteria and other living things.

Plesiosaurs
A group of swimming, aquatic reptiles from the Mesozoic era, all of which had two pairs of wing-like flippers. The group includes short-necked species with large heads as well as long-necked kinds with small heads.

Predator
A carnivorous (meat-eating) animal that survives by catching, killing and eating other animals. Wolves, tigers and sharks are all predators, but so are ladybirds and robins.

Pterosaurs
A group of winged reptiles, closely related to dinosaurs, that evolved in the Triassic period and died out at the end of the Cretaceous period. Pterosaurs had furry bodies and were probably warm-blooded.

Quills
Long structures that grow out of the skin of some animals. Some quills – like those of porcupines – are sharply pointed and are used for defence. Bird feathers have a stiff central shaft known as a quill.

Reptiles
The name usually given to the group of four-legged, scaly-skinned animals with a backbone that includes turtles, lizards, snakes and crocodilians. Most reptiles are cold-blooded, but some such as dinosaurs (including birds) and pterosaurs, were warm-blooded and furry or feathery.

Sauropods
The group of long-necked plant-eating dinosaurs that includes Diplodocus and Brachiosaurus. Most sauropods were enormous and some kinds were the biggest land animals of all time.

Saurischians
The group of dinosaurs that possesses a particularly long, flexible neck, including both theropods (including birds) and sauropods and their relatives.

Serrated
When the edge of an object possesses a set of tooth-like points like a saw, it is described as serrated. The edges of many leaves and the teeth of some carnivorous animals are serrated.

Triassic
The section of time (known as a period) between the Permian and Jurassic periods. It extended from 250 to 199 million years ago. Dinosaurs first appeared during the Triassic.

Vertebrae
The collective name for the bones that form the backbone – each of which is individually called a vertebra. Humans have 33 vertebrae, while long-bodied animals like snakes have more than 200.

Warm-blooded
The popular name given to animals that generate and keep heat inside their bodies. Mammals and birds are warm-blooded, but so are some insects and fish. There is evidence that at least some Mesozoic dinosaurs were warm-blooded.

Wingspan
The name given to the distance between the two wingtips when the wings are outstretched.

CREDITS

The publishers would like to thank the following sources for their kind permission to reproduce the pictures in this book. Every effort has been made to correctly acknowledge and contact the source and/or copyright holder of each picture, and Carlton Books Limited apologizes for any unintentional errors or omissions, which will be corrected in future editions of this book.

PICTURE CREDITS:

p.4 Dr Darren Naish • p.10: (t) Bettmann/Corbis (b) Crazytang/istockphoto.com • p.11: sahua d/shutterstock • p.13: Computer Earth/shutterstock • p.14: Ulrich Mueller/shutterstock • p.15: John Carnemolla/shutterstock • p.16: Johan Swanepoel/shutterstock • p.18: Eric Isselée/shutterstock • p.20: Eric Isselée/shutterstock • p.21: RichLindie/istockphoto.com • p.22: Sheila Terry/Science Photo Library • p.25: Julius T Csotonyi/Science Photo Library • p.27: Sylvain Cordier (Imagebank)/Getty Images • p.28: Ingus Rukis/shutterstock • p.29: Vladimir Sazonov/shutterstock • p.30: Ian Tragen/shutterstock • p.31: R. Gino Santa Maria/shutterstock • p.32: Paul D Stewart/Science Photo Library • p.33: (t) Eric Isselée/shutterstock • p.34: Olemac/shutterstock • p.37: tatniz/shutterstock • p.38: Wolfe Larry/shutterstock • p.39: Photodisc • p.43: Julia Mihatsch/shutterstock • p.44: July Flower/shutterstock • p.46: FloridaStock/shutterstock • p.48: Four Oaks/shutterstock • p.51: Joesboy/istockphoto.com • p.52: iPics/shutterstock • p.57: alexal/shutterstock • p.58: JoeLena/istockphoto.com: • p.59: Louie Psihoyos (Science Faction Jewels)/Getty Images • p.61: Eric Isselée/shutterstock • p.63 Pete Saloutos/shutterstock • p.65: vedderman123/shutterstock • p.66: Andrew Kerr/shutterstock • p.67: EdeWolf/istockphoto.com • p.69: AYImages/istockphoto.com • p.71: (t/l) Michael Marsland/Yale University • p.71: (t/r) bobainsworth/istockphoto.com • p.71: (b/l) Louie Psihoyos/Corbis • p.74: Jay Mitchell • p.75: shrizzine/istockphoto.com • p.77: Oleksii Abramov/shutterstock • p.79: (t) stickyworm/istockphoto.com • p.79: (b) Nagel Photography/shutterstock • p.81: Four Oaks/shutterstock • p.82: Philip O'Brien/shutterstock • p.84: Louie Psihoyos/Corbis • p.86: Messier111/istockphoto.com • p.87: Sue Robinson/shutterstock • p.89: Geanina Bechea/shutterstock • p.91: Volodymyr Goinyk/shutterstock • p.93: Eric Isselée/shutterstock • p.94: APaterson/shutterstock • p.95: Kjersti Joergensen/shutterstock • p.97: Kathie Atkinson/(Oxford Scientific) Getty Images • p.98: Ralf Juergen Kraft/shutterstock • p.100: Rob Wilson/shutterstock • p.101: loong/istockphoto.com • p.107: jocrebbin/istockphoto.com • p.108: Gerrit_de_Vries/shutterstock • p.110: Michael C. Gray/shutterstock • p.111: bierchen/shutterstock • p.112: Ralf Juergen Kraft/shutterstock • p.114: B.G. Smith/shutterstock • p.115: Lasse Kristensen/shutter:stock • p.117: Chris Twine/shutterstock • p.119: Anna Kaewkhammul/shutterstock • p.122: loong/shutterstock • p.123 ramihalim/istockphoto.com • p.125: Daniel Herbert/shutterstock • p.126: James Thew/shutterstock • p.127: Linda Bucklin/shutterstock